10-5-70

# THERE'S
# NO
# OTHER
# WAY

# THERE'S NO OTHER WAY

Ernest A. Fitzgerald

Nashville • ABINGDON ⓟ PRESS • New York

THERE'S NO OTHER WAY

*Copyright © 1970 by Abingdon Press*

*ISBN 0-687-41633-7*

*Library of Congress Catalog Card Number: 75-124753*

SET UP, PRINTED, AND BOUND BY
THE PARTHENON PRESS, AT NASHVILLE,
TENNESSEE, UNITED STATES OF AMERICA

*To  Frances*

whose untiring loyalty and abiding love
have made my life an exciting adventure
and our home "a hiding place from the
wind and a shelter from the storm."

Problems of society, personal problems —where does the solution lie for the continuing dilemmas of mankind? Jesus has spoken words of timeless wisdom in the Sermon on the Mount. These words, says Ernest Fitzgerald, are not one of the options confronting today's world, but man's only alternative for survival.

To accept God's intended plan for human existence is to overcome frustration and despair and to gain victory in life. To show the workings of this plan in contemporary life, Dr. Fitzgerald considers perplexities common to every life. Happiness—where is it found? Morality —how is it defined? Love—how can it overcome?

Examine with Dr. Fitzgerald the difficulties of any clear-cut answer to questions such as these. Then turn with him

(*Continued on back flap*) ......, and Film Commission and serving on the Commission on Christian Social Concerns, the Board of Pensions, and the Committee on Methodist Information.

Active in community affairs, Dr. Fitzgerald has been a member of many civic clubs as well as a member of the Board of Trustees of Pfeiffer College. He serves as a member of the Board of Visitors of Duke University.

Dr. Fitzgerald has received degrees from Western Carolina College (A.B.), Duke Divinity School (B.D.), and High Point College (D.D.).

# Foreword

Anyone who experienced the waves of oratory which swept across the land during presidential primaries and subsequent campaigns of recent years, anyone who watches television documentaries, or listens to a head of state mold the reactions of his populace with carefully chosen phrases, knows that there has never been a time when the spoken word was more influential than it is now. Style and idiom have changed in many instances, and the approach is more "low key" than the old hortatory eruption, but the power of public speaking to ignite the mind, sway the emotions, and marshal the will lives on in undiminished glory. Thomas Carlyle uttered quaint but timely words, needed especially for those in our time who question the role of a person with an audience: "I wish that speaking man could find the point

again, *for there is need of him yet!*" There was—
and is.

It seems absurd that intelligent Christians
would doubt the importance of preaching at a
moment when the Church is struggling to affirm
its ancient identity and to make contemporary its
presentation of Jesus Christ. The pulpit and pew
compose a forum still more persuasive and power-
ful than any other in our society. As Dr. Harold
Bosley has well said, "If the Gospel is the central
gift of the Church, then the proclamation of it is
as important as ever." [1]

People are still going to church (in most im-
pressive numbers) where the man in the pulpit is
biblical, lucid, interesting, and helpful—and
where he deeply and passionately believes in the
importance of the message he is seeking to deliver.
There is a new pulpit oratory, neither stilted nor
ornate, more conversational and dialogical than the
old, but just as vivid and telling. For some of us,
this new form for an ancient craft is difficult—a
fact that makes it all the more exciting to discover
a modern preacher who has mastered it.

Ernest A. Fitzgerald, standing responsibly in a
pulpit made important by masters like Mark

[1] Harold A. Bosley, "The Role of Preaching in American History." Introductory essay in *Preaching in American History*, ed.
DeWitte Holland (Nashville: Abingdon Press, 1969), p. 34.

Depp and Kenneth Goodson, is a young minister who combines sensitive understanding of the Gospel's meaning for an age of revolution with informed and focused logic and winsome, persuasive clarity. Son and brother of able preachers, he carefully prepares his sermons and then delivers them with consummate effectiveness. It is worthy of note that his preaching is only one influential part of Ernest Fitzgerald's ministry—a vigorous and memorable movement in a total symphony of pastoral service. He is responding with distinction to the difficult challenge of making a large institutional church into a center of meaningful ministry and vital Christian witness in a highly secularized moment of human history.

As one who has had frequent opportunities to rejoice over Dr. Fitzgerald's accomplishments, and who is familar with both his ability and integrity, I deem it an honor to commend these excellent sermons to the wide and appreciative readership they deserve. I am confident that they will prove to be but the pleasant beginning of a still wider influence on the part of the good minister of Jesus Christ who preached them to his people.

EARL G. HUNT, JR.

# Ernest A. Fitzgerald

"The heart of the Christian proclamation can be found in the Sermon on the Mount. It is not, as we have often imagined, the speculation of a long-ago dreamer. Here, instead, is a realistic description of the Creator's design for human survival. The principles set forth here are written into the scheme of things, and they do not require our endorsement to make them valid."

—*The Author*

From Chapter Two: *Happiness—The Way It Is*

"Let me tell you how it is. You are chasing the wrong things. Here is what you are really after, and here is the way to find it."

From Chapter Five: *Morality—The Way It Is*

"Suppose we ask honestly, not what economics, custom, or law requires, but what does love require? Jesus indicated that a world of darkness would be transformed into a world of light. Do you suppose He was right?"

From Chapter Ten: *Friendship—The Way It Is.*

"Jesus insisted that we begin with ourselves in seeking the acceptance of our brother. We cannot hope to have the respect of our neighbor unless we have earned it."

ABINGDON PRESS

# *Preface*

So often these days the Christian faith is being presented as one of many options confronting modern man. The invitation is to "try God" as one would experiment with a new medicine which may or may not have therapeutic value. Proclaiming the Good News in such an uncertain way, however, only contributes to the dilemma of the uncommitted. The day has come when we need to affirm clearly that this ancient message is the proven prescription for the ills of contemporary life.

The heart of the Christian proclamation can be found in the Sermon on the Mount. It is not, as we have often imagined, the speculations of a long-ago dreamer. Here, instead, is a realistic description of the Creator's design for human survival. The principles stated here are written into the scheme of things and do not require our endorsement to make them valid. Our failure to accept them simply results in our continued frustration and despair.

The chapters in this little volume represent one man's attempt to examine the Sermon on the Mount from this vantage point. In many ways it constitutes the spiritual autobiography of one who seeks to identify these principles and test them in the light of his own experience. The intent is to add another voice to that innumerable host of witnesses who are discovering that for our time and place—There's No Other Way!

I am indebted to my parents, the Reverend and Mrs. J. B. Fitzgerald, who first translated into life for me the truths of the Sermon on the Mount; to Mrs. O. Dewey Smith and Mrs. Matt McBrayer, who have offered invaluable assistance in the preparation and editing of the manuscript; to Mrs. David Lewis, whose skill as a secretary is unsurpassed; to Bishop Earl G. Hunt, Jr., for his guidance and counsel; and to Mr. and Mrs. Ralph M. Stockton, Sr., whose gentle spirits encouraged me to assemble this little book. I am especially grateful to the staff and members of Centenary United Methodist Church, who constantly inspire and challenge me to reach for higher things.

ERNEST A. FITZGERALD
Winston-Salem, North Carolina

# Contents

# The Way It Is

Matthew 7:24-29

A national newsmagazine reported recently that the Flat Earth Society, based in Dover, England, has been forced to revise its theories on the shape of the earth following the Apollo 8 mission to the moon. In the late 1950s a half-dozen good-natured dissenters met in London to organize an effort to combat what they called the " 'absurd' round-earth theory." Under the leadership of Samuel Shenton, a 65-year-old retired sign painter, the organization has grown to well over a hundred members. The other day, however, the society announced that it would have to reconsider its position and concede that "the earth is circular." But, they maintained, it is "not globe-shaped. The orbits [made by spacemen around] the earth were simply circular flights, like flying around the rim of a saucer."

I was a bit amused when I read this announcement. I am not greatly surprised, however, to discover that there are still "holdouts" on what appears to be clearly evident. As a matter of fact, most of us in one way or another are refugees from the truth. Probably in this regard we bear a kinship with each other. There often seems to be a time lag between the discovery of facts and our acceptance of them. We tend to revise our positions slowly, holding on to traditional conclusions long after the evidence demands a new verdict.

Perhaps the place where this is most apparent has been the credibility gap between science and religion across the years. In 1632 the church condemned Galileo for contending, among other things, that the earth was a globe. Yet more than one hundred years before, Magellan's sailors had circumnavigated the earth; and ships were roaming the seas, finding no end to their world. The famed "Scopes Monkey Trial" in Tennessee is another case in point. The book of Genesis and modern science were thrown into a conflict which we have later decided did not exist. Of course, the gap between science and religion has narrowed rapidly in recent years. Intelligent Christianity and intelligent science are clearly compatible today. Any conflict between them is more a matter of myth than fact.

Unfortunately, the time lag between the discovery of truth and our acceptance of it has not diminished with equal rapidity in other areas. Unlike the good-natured dissenters of the Flat Earth Society, our unyielding resistance in these areas is stubborn, defiant, and sometimes ill-tempered. While Sam Shenton's holdout on the Apollo 8 affirmations is probably harmless, our unwillingness to accept the truth in other areas can be dangerous and tragic. Let us explore this possibility, and in doing so attempt to awaken some areas of thought which may make our lives more meaningful.

# I

In April of 1968, the General Conference of The United Methodist Church challenged Methodist people everywhere to an intensive effort to bind up the open wounds of estrangement and strife in our world. The Conference suggested that fundamental in this effort should be a renewed study of the Sermon on the Mount. In my judgment, this is imperative. There is a grave danger that the church may fall into a social activism devoid of

17

biblical and theological foundations. No ship dares to sail without bearing and direction. The General Conference suggested that the Sermon on the Mount become the chart and compass for United Methodism's current voyage. Surely this proposal demands consideration.

One thing about modern man's evaluation of the Sermon on the Mount troubles me. We see it as a nice little treatise proposing the visionary ideals of an ancient dreamer. We are willing to accept the fact that the ideas apparent in it are beautiful expressions of what ought to be, but most of us doubt that they are practical. Recently, I have been reflecting on this thought. Perhaps the Sermon on the Mount is not just a suggestion of the way life ought to work; perhaps it is a description of the only way it will work. That puts these first few chapters of Matthew in an entirely new light, does it not? It means that Jesus was telling it—not the way it ought to be—but the way it is. Think for a moment about that possibility.

It would be strange, indeed, if there were no abiding principles undergirding the moral and spiritual world. Certainly nowhere else is this true. Consider mathematics, for instance. The multiplication tables are not suggestions of the way things ought to be; rather, they constitute a description of the way things are. They do not demand our vote of confidence in order to be valid. Or, for another example, imagine someone opening a physics book, reading the law of gravity, and commenting, "Isn't that nice? But I don't particularly like that law so I will use another." That never happens, does it? And the reason it doesn't happen is that we have come to respect the statement of the law of gravity as a description of the way it is and not what we would like it to be.

We have long since concluded that there is nothing really new in the Sermon on the Mount. Jesus simply distilled the sum total of human wisdom on these matters and laid it down in a dozen or so concise principles. He was not legislating a new way of life; rather, he was interpreting life as it is. If this is true, then our attempt to organize holdout societies to protest what he said is absurd and ridiculous. The people who heard Jesus speak recognized this. Our writer ends the sermon with one significant phrase: "Jesus taught them as One having authority and not as the scribes." The scribes, you remember, were the religious lawyers of their day. They kept trying to make the rules for life. Jesus took a different direction. He made no attempt to make the rules. He simply revealed the nature of life. "This is the way," he said. Despite our protests to the contrary,

19

the collective experience of mankind validates his description.

## II

Now suppose for a moment that what we are saying is true, that the Sermon on the Mount is a description of the way things are going to work. This may account for the suffering that you and I endure when we live in conflict with it.

Ralph Sockman tells of a lady who once said to Lord Byron, after Byron's life had ground to a halt from undisciplined living, "You ought not to have declared war on the world. It's an impossibility. I tried it myself when I was young, but it's impossible." There is a hint of something here that is vitally important. If the Sermon on the Mount is an account of the way things are, then to declare war on it is to invite disaster.

I have always enjoyed woodworking. Across the years I have discovered that every piece of timber has its distinctive grain. When you clamp it in a vise for planning, you had just as well recognize this. If you work against the grain, you will never get the wood smooth. It's like declaring war on the world. If you work "with the grain," nature will work with you. Oppose the grain and you are inviting trouble.

Do you suppose this is one of the reasons we have so much difficulty in getting things to work out right in our lives? We are running against the grain. Billy Sunday, the fiery evangelist of a previous generation, was often accused of creating turmoil everywhere he went. "The trouble with you, Billy," said a friend, "is that you are always rubbing the dog's fur the wrong way." Billy, you remember, made a whimsical and masterful observation in reply. "It is also possible that the dog is turned the wrong way." That is a crude way of putting it, but the point is clear. Life in opposition to its intended direction is disastrous. In the end our lives may have to be redirected to conform with life's intended plan.

One day on the outskirts of a little town, Jesus met a young man who asked him to describe the way life worked. Jesus told him, and, the biblical writer declares, the young man went away sorrowfully. I imagine that there was more to that story than we have in the Bible. Apparently the young fellow was extremely influential. (We have since labeled him as the rich young ruler.) Perhaps the disciples said to Jesus, "Go after him; don't let him get away; we can use a man of influence on our side. Go tell him that you will change things for him." Here the record is absolutely clear. Jesus let him go, but not because he wanted to. The

21

writer indicates that Jesus had great compassion for him. The fact was that Jesus could not change the rules. The only thing he could do was to tell the young man the way it had to be.

Most of us at one time or another have declared war on the world. We write our own rules at times and take a beating until it gets through to us that our rules are written for the way we want life to work and not the way it is going to work. We discover then what the Flat Earth Society is now admitting. There is sometimes a difference between what we believe about the facts and what the facts are! Ultimately, it is we who suffer and not the truth.

## III

There is an alternate side to this that we must not neglect. If the Sermon on the Mount is a statement of the way things are, then obedience to it is the way to life.

There is an old word in church terminology that has been badly abused. That word is *surrender*. In its usual definition it is a word describing weakness and defeat. David MacLennan tells about a little boy who was asked to write a definition of a Christian. "Christians," he said, "are mild, weak, and quiet people who never fight or

talk back. Daddy is a Christian. Mother is not."
Well, hurrah for Mother! If these are the sole
qualifications of a Christian, then we need to take
a look at that band of militant followers of Jesus
who changed the world in a single century. They
were surrendered men; but surrender as it is used
in the New Testament does not mean defeat. It
means cooperation, and that is entirely different.

The King James Version of the Bible contains
an interesting phrase in the story of Paul's conversion that is not always included in other versions. Paul was on his way down to Damascus,
breathing threats of violence against the Christians
there. Somewhere on the way he had a vision and
heard a divine voice speaking to him. "Saul, Saul"
(this, of course, was Paul's pre-Christian name),
"why persecutest thou me? . . . It is hard . . . to
kick against the pricks." Or, to put it another way,
"It's tough, going against the grain." The story
goes on to describe the transformation that took
place that day on the Damascus road. A miserable,
tormented man was changed into one of the most
vibrant, vigorous, and dynamic lives in history.
The heart of Paul's conversion was simply that
Paul ceased fighting God's will and surrendered
to the intended direction of his life.

For many years I read this story only as history,
giving little thought to its meaning. Then one day

I saw my own reflection in it. Separated by two thousand years, I felt a kinship with that man who made his way down to Damascus. I watched him as he walked along, and suddenly it occurred to me that clearly mirrored in that miserable, lonely man is the image of all of us who are holdouts on the truth. His problem is our problem. Perhaps his answer is our answer, too. Some of us have attempted to walk with him and to live life as he lived it after that moment on the Damascus road. We have managed to match his life only in a very limited way, but to the degree that we have, life has been radiantly different.

Victory through surrender—this is a paradox that the world never seems to understand. There is a way to life that knows no ultimate defeat. It yields to no adversity. That life comes only to those who have surrendered, those who cooperate with what life is intended to be. The description of that life is registered here in the Sermon on the Mount. We need to study it again. For some of us it could be the beginning of a new day.

# Happiness—The Way It Is

*Matthew 5:1-11*

For a number of years Joseph Fort Newton wrote a column for one of the Philadelphia papers. One day, he related, he was standing at a window looking out over a lovely garden near his home. Just outside a little boy was intently chasing a small insect. It was a beautiful creature. It flitted gently through the brilliant sunshine and lighted softly on a nearby flower. Suddenly the boy leaped from behind a shrub and grasped the insect tightly in his hand. Across his face flashed a look of triumph, and then came a cry of agony. He opened his hand to see his prize. Instead of finding the lovely little creature he had pursued, he saw only some crumpled wings and the dirty smear of a disarranged bumblebee.

25

## THERE'S NO OTHER WAY

There is something penetrating in this little parable. Many times we go after things with frenzied effort, and, when we finally run them down, they turn out to be quite different from what we expected. So much of life is wasted this way. Our hands were not made to clench bumblebees. Any attempt to do so is a perversion of God's intended scheme of things.

There might be some value in pausing long enough to think about this. We assume that man is the master of creation, and that whatever he wants he can have. Suppose, however, that the things we want are incompatible with our natures. Despite the fact that they are attractive, in reality, they diminish life. How much more meaningful life could be if we could sort out these things and cease to spend our lives searching for them.

Apparently, Jesus was aware of this need. To him, the greatest tragedy of all was a wasted life. He must have seen man racing along chasing the illusion of some beautiful things, unaware that their attractiveness was deceptive. So one day Jesus sat down with his people and said to them, "Let me tell you how it is. You are chasing the wrong things. Here is what you are really after, and here is the way to find it." Thus he gave to us these immortal little passages called the Beatitudes. The treasures of these verses are inexhaustible, but two or three things about them appear readily evident.

# I

First, *Jesus described the most cherished possession of life.* Almost any commentary that you read on the Beatitudes will translate the word *blessed* as meaning happy. This, of course, is only a haphazard translation and may even be misleading. What we mean by the word *happiness,* and what the ancient scribes of the New Testament intended by the word *blessed* are probably two different things.

I picked up an anthology of quotations the other day and ran down the pages under the topic of happiness. I was surprised to discover so many cynical references to it. Most of them suggested that happiness is a mirage which appears real until you get to it. I began to wonder why so many people who have written on this theme are so disillusioned about it. Finally, it occurred to me that what they meant by happiness is impossible as a human achievement. They understood the word to mean the absence of struggle; a state of being where all pressure, tension, and striving is suspended. However, such a circumstance is incompatible with the nature of our being. If man is to find any happiness at all, he has to find it under pressure. He lives in a world that will never let him rest. All of us are the potential victims of calamity and disaster. We awake every morning under the load of life and retire in the evening still burdened.

I heard of a family who had moved from the Methodist to the Episcopal church. One of the little girls was asked why the family had changed churches. "Mother," she said brightly, "likes the Episcopal *lethargy* better." Well, I doubt if Episcopalians have it much easier than Methodists. Man was born to struggle. That's the way it is.

Some commentaries suggest that the word blessed comes from an old Greek word describing a joy that has its secret within itself. It is an inner state of contentment, an untouchable serenity. The Beatitudes refer to a state of gladness that is independent of pain, sorrow, or loss; a kind of joy that nothing in life or death can destroy. On this level, blessedness takes on a new meaning. It means not the happiness that results from the absence of struggle, but the happiness that endures through the struggle. The first is impossible in this world, man being what he is and creation being what it is. If there is any happiness at all in this world, it must be the latter.

## II

Second, *Jesus said that this happiness can be a present possession.* William Barclay in *The Gospel of Matthew,* has an interesting insight in his commentary on the Beatitudes. He notes that when the phrase *blessed are* appears in most English translations the word *are* is usually in italics. This, of course, indicates that there is no equivalent word in the Greek or Hebrew, and that the translators have added the word to bring out the meaning of the verse. He goes on to suggest that a proper translation might well be *"O the blessedness of the poor in spirit,"* or *"O the blessedness of the merciful."* "This," he says, "means that Jesus was not talking about something reserved for the future. He was talking about a happiness which can be had here and now."

So much of the traditional interpretation of the Christian faith indicates that whatever possessions the Christian may have are reserved for the hereafter. I asked a friend the other day, as we were running along trying to keep up with far too heavy a schedule of appointments and duties, "When are things going to slow down a bit?" "In about ten days," he said. "Of course, I said that ten years ago." That's the way most of us feel about happiness. It's just over the hill, about ten days

29

away. But if happiness means what most of us take it to mean, it's farther away than that. The happiness Jesus talked about is possible now. It is a present possession, available in the middle of this pressurized, frenzied world in which we live.

Our thesis in this study of the Sermon on the Mount is that Jesus is telling it not the way we would like it to be, but the way it is. Is not what we are saying here an affirmation of this idea? Who has ever managed to gain release from the struggles of life? That person down the street from you, young or old, rich or poor, is loaded down with cares. His problem is different from yours or mine, but it is just as nettlesome, and, to him, just as difficult. If he has any joy at all, it is in spite of his load and not because of his release from it.

It is precisely at this point that the secret of the truly radiant lives of history is revealed. From what we are able to learn of their biographies, the great people of the world were not exempt from the kind of life the rest of us face. They were out there on the front lines taking whatever life had to offer. Though the storms raged on the outside, there was calm within. "This," said Jesus, "is the only kind of happiness that never crumbles or stings when you possess it." Happiness is not something you have in your hands; it is something you carry in your heart.

## III

Finally, *Jesus declared that this possession comes by indirection.* You can imagine Jesus in the marketplace talking with his people. Their faces reflected eager hearts. Everyone is interested in happiness. "Now," Jesus said, "this is the kind of contentment you are seeking—the tranquillity of the soul. And how do you find it? Let me tell it like it is: Blessed are those who depend on God. Blessed are those who seek righteousness. Blessed are those who make peace. Blessed are those who hold to a principle," and so on down the list. "Happiness is not something you can have directly. It is something that comes to you as the result of another kind of pursuit."

Seneca, the Greek philosopher and contemporary of Jesus, made a comment that contained an element of truth. "Happiness consists in not departing from nature." A happy life is one that is in accordance with what it is intended to be. We should never miss the meaning of these words. Life lived the way it was intended to be lived automatically results in that inner peace which the world cannot give or take away. Where is the man who has ever found peace except by living within the intended scheme of things?

Disraeli once made a speech before Parliament

in which he said something that touched a tender nerve, and the halls came alive with shouts of anger. The members hooted at him. He tried to speak, but his audience shouted him down. Disraeli quietly closed his book and waited for the noise to subside. With complete composure, in the dead silence, he made one final comment. "The time will come when you will hear me." This is exactly what we are saying here. Disraeli believed that what he had to say was backed by the eternal scheme of things. He could endure the storm on the outside, because he was sustained by the inner knowledge that he was going the way things would turn out to be.

A long time ago, a man trod the streets of little villages in a faraway corner of the world. His mind had grasped the precious secrets about the way man and his world are made. "Brothers, listen to me. God intended us to be humble, sympathetic, reconcilers, morally pure, etc. Live life as God intended it, and you can have the peace of God now. That's the way it is." The Beatitudes are worth a lot of study for those who are searching for new life. Have you considered them recently? There's no other way!

# Power—The Way It Is

*Matthew 5:5*

An article appeared in the February 24, 1957 edition of *The New York Times* with the intriguing title, "Even Dogs Get Ulcers Leading a People's Life." Apparently the article was a report on some experiments in which animals were subjected to the tensions of human environment. While I have no knowledge of these experiments, I would guess that the title suggests a valid conclusion.

The human situation is always one of tension. In the first pages of the Bible the writers recognized this. Man, in the Genesis account of creation, was commissioned to subdue and master his environment. From that day until this, he has been struggling with this commission. It involves

33

both a collective and an individual effort. From the beginning man has wrestled with his world and sought to understand it. His efforts to conquer disease, to utilize natural resources, and to master space are all demonstrations of this. His tension has also been personal. One by one, we face our own little worlds filled with the grim facts of life. We have to deal with anxiety, failure, tragedy, conflict, loss, disease, and death. Anyone who has lived long is fully aware that life is a series of succeeding crises. We move from one to the other, often without letup in between.

In conquering life, our critical need is for strength. Almost every day someone out there in the thick of things asks a plaintive question: "I wonder if I will have the strength to bear the load?" People ask this question when confronted with some gigantic problem. Young people wonder about it as they look out upon the hard realitities of their world. Older people, scarred and battered by rigorous tribulation, raise the question when facing the bleak possibilities of the future. It is an age-old question. The strength to meet the tension of life and master it is the pressing concern of all men.

In the Sermon on the Mount, Jesus faced this question and addressed himself to it. His answer seems strangely unrealistic. "Blessed are the meek, for they shall inherit the earth." For centuries men have eagerly read this passage. Man wants to subdue his earth, to master life, rather than be mastered by it. However, most of us have trouble with the method Jesus suggested—meekness. Either Jesus was wrong in what he said, or we do not understand him. We ask an earnest question: "Have the meek ever inherited anything?" Perhaps we can deal with this question by some observations on the nature of meekness as Jesus intended it.

## I

Most of our problem with meekness is in the matter of definition. Bible translators have always struggled with the difficulty of conveying exact meanings when moving from one language to another. This is especially true here. Webster describes meekness, among other definitions, as being *tamely submissive,* or *easily imposed upon.* It is this latter definition which usually comes to our minds when we use the word *meekness.* It is a kind of Uriah Heep humility, a spineless, spiritless resignation. This definition of meekness, however, does not prevail in equivalent words in other languages.

A study of this word in other languages is interesting. The Greek word for meekness means far more than the English word now implies. Barclay, in his commentary *The Gospel of Matthew*, points out that Aristotle defined virtue as the median between two extremes. For instance, between miserliness and wastefulness there is a midpoint that is good. Barclay says that Aristotle associated meekness with anger. It is the midpoint between too little and too much. In other words, meekness to Aristotle was the proper regulation of explosive impulses.

This is why the Greeks' word for meekness was often used to describe wild animals—especially horses—that had been domesticated. The fiery and unruly passions of the beast have been focused and channeled into useful purposes. The word was used for an animal that learned to accept control and to sublimate its unruly power into constructive uses. Barclay goes on to point out that the Greeks often contrasted their word for meekness with another word, which means loftyheartedness. Here meekness connotes a true humility, the kind of humility a person has when he recognizes his limitations and is willing to be guided and controlled.

It would seem to me that, against this background, we are forced to redefine the usual meaning of meekness when it is used in a Christian context. Set within the total message of Jesus, we might well define "the meek" as those who have allowed their passions, powers, and explosive impulses to be brought under the control of God and thus to be used in keeping with God's will. Harold Bosley describes the meek as the spiritually trained people who are continually hearing and cooperating with the will of God. "These are the people," said Jesus, "who inherit the earth, who have the mastery of life." I raise the question now, "Was Jesus telling it like it is? Do the meek inherit the earth?" One way to answer this question is to test it in the light of human experience.

## II

Look for a moment at the biblical evidence supporting this proposition that the meek inherit the earth. Let us use one of the best-known stories in the Bible. The day the armies of the Israelites faced the legions of the Philistines was one of great peril. The Philistines had a warrior—a giant of a man—named Goliath, who cut a wide path wherever he went. His strength was so massive that he was arrogant, proud, and undisciplined. He was strong enough to be careless. He could blunder along, pushing aside everything in his path. The Israelites were frightened by his strength. They had no one courageous enough to face him, save one little shepherd boy named David. David had no great strength. But he had a sling, a good eye, and a strong arm, and he put these things together. He brought all his powers to focus on the act of hurling a single stone. Goliath died that day on the field of battle, and David's hand was raised in victory. Let us not get lost in the literal interpretation of the story. I do not think that God ordered the death of Goliath. What we have here is a parable about the way things are. Strength and might have a way of overestimating themselves into oblivion, leaving the meek to inherit the earth.

The finest example of this is evident in the life of Jesus. Jesus was a man who focused all his powers into a cooperative venture with God. He was not without anger, as the crooked money changers in the temple would testify. Yet his anger was always constructively directed and in keeping with the will of God. He was not easily pushed around, nor was he tamely submissive. Look at him the night he stood before Pilate. Pilate had the power of the Roman legions on his side. There was every reason to believe that the militant would inherit the earth. The Roman soldiers had subdued the Jews, and the Jews had never been easy to conquer. The Jews had attempted to break their bondage, going sometimes to the point of revolt; but Rome with its massive strength always managed to crush the revolt. That night, when Jesus stood before Pilate as one man against an empire, it appeared that He did not have a chance. But Jesus had behind him one strength which the Romans underestimated; he was completely surrendered to the control of God. The record is now clear. Pilate is gone, without admiration or followers. The "meek and gentle" Jesus has inherited the earth.

This theme runs all through the Bible. The mighty men who have moved with careless abandon, intoxicated by their own strength, out of control, oblivious to the will of God, have all fallen into the dust. The little people, aware of their limitations, but allowing their lives to be controlled from above—the meek—inherited the earth.

## III

The story is the same everywhere. The meek master life. The reason, of course, is not difficult to understand. Man has no strength of his own. Every ounce of power he can claim is given to him when he meets the conditions God has established as necessary for receiving power. Our physical strength is a good example. We do not manufacture that. We simply eat the right foods, exercise properly, follow good habits, and nature supplies the strength as a result. The strong man is the man who meets the conditions for strength. The meek, then, are those who surrender their lives to the direction of God. As a consequence, the strength of God stands behind them.

There is a sharp debate going on in our world today over the problem of morality. It is a heated controversy in which the real issues are not always considered. Each side is trying to force its opinion on the other. The one question which is sometimes ignored is this: "What does God intend?" Morality, in its highest meaning, is not relative to social custom, nor is it man's imposed regulation. Morality is what God intends. It is wider than the debate on sex. Morality touches every facet of man's behavior, all the way from matters of social conduct down to his personal eating and drinking habits. What God intends is morally right. What God does not intend is morally wrong. Life is so arranged that man, when his life is in conflict with God's intent, can count on absolute and certain defeat. But life in obedience to God's intent shall not be overcome.

There is a story going around these days about a truck driver who went into a restaurant for dinner and ordered a steak. Before he could eat it, a half-dozen hipsters roared up on their motocycles and walked into the dining room. They were dressed in dirty leather jackets, and had long unkempt hair. They took the man's steak, cut it into six pieces, and ate it. The driver said nothing. He simply paid the bill and walked out. One of the fellows said to the others, "That man couldn't talk; he didn't say a word." Another said, "He couldn't fight; he didn't lift a hand." A waiter nearby overheard and remarked, "I would say he couldn't drive. On his way out of the parking lot he ran over six motorcycles." Now this is not an exact illustration of what I have been saying. God does not seek revenge upon those who are in opposition to him, but it is true that creation has sufficient strength to sustain its purpose.

What does God intend? Have we considered this recently with reference to our lives? It has bearing on our personal conduct, our relationships with others, the way we run our businesses, and even on our national and international affairs. God's intent is the way all men finally have to go. Any other course is a disaster.

## IV

Let me, therefore, set before you a final thought. If life for you does not mean what it should mean, if you are being battered and beaten by the storms of life, your trouble is not that you are living in a *people's* world. All of us share that experience. It could be that you are not going at life in God's way. Jesus promised that the meek—those who are submitted to God's control—inherit the earth. "Don't knock it until you have tried it."

# Work—The Way It Is

*Matthew 5:13-16*

Several years ago, Emil Brunner, one of the distinguished theologians of the twentieth century, wrote *I Believe in the Living*, a series of sermons on the Apostles' Creed. In the final sermon of that series he made this statement: "At the beginning of the Second World War, many of us looked upon our lives as finished and since then take every day we live as a special gift of God." This statement had particular significance coming from Brunner. He spent the war years near to the heart of war itself. Like many other Europeans, he lived each day never sure of tomorrow.

Sometimes it takes a personal encounter with danger to make us aware of the precious quality of life. I have a friend who suffered a severe illness several years ago. The outcome was in question for weeks. Shortly after his recovery, he said, "Nothing in my lifetime has so sensitized me to the emptiness of my life. Reflections from a sickbed forced me to the clear realization that there is a difference between living and being alive. I have spent most of my life racing around on the monotonous treadmill of existence without purpose or meaningful direction." A lot of us, if we are absolutely honest about it, feel this way at times. For some of us, it is the chronic atmosphere of our lives.

No generation has given more evidence of being fed up with life than our own. This attitude is apparent among the haves as well as the have-nots. There does not seem to be much difference in our zest for life, regardless of our social or economic status. Many of us have that tired, listless look in our eyes. The older generation of our society has tried everything, been everywhere, and is still restless. Younger people are trying the same things their elders tried but in other ways, and the results are little different. The blunt truth about it all is that a lot of us are alive, but we are really not living.

Why is it that we must hear the thunder of screaming bombs and feel the cold breath of the

Grim Reaper before we face up to the emptiness of our lives? Is it not possible for us, even in this day of relative prosperity and safety, to consider our predicament? Some of us are doing this, I think, and are searching for a prescription to cure the dull, drab character of life. For any who may have this quest in mind, let me suggest some words from the Sermon on the Mount. "You are the salt of the earth. But if the salt has lost its savor, it is good for nothing. You don't light a candle and place it under a bushel. You put it on a candlestick." What did Jesus mean by these words? Consider them for a moment.

# I

First, think about the passage itself. Most of us have read these verses many times, and almost always we interpret them as describing the role of a Christian in his world. Jesus seems to be speaking directly to his followers. There was a gathering storm on the horizon. Rome had reached unprecedented glory, but there were those who could see troubled times ahead. The world was beginning to feel the threat of possible calamity. There were many thoughtful people—as in our own time—who were apprehensive about the future.

Against such a cloud-covered background Jesus had called together a small band of followers and given them a mission. "You are the hope of the world, the light for men who travel in darkness." The metaphor here has many ramifications, but basically it applies to the church and the role it has always had in its world—a handful of people turned loose in the darkness of the earth, spreading light until the darkness is dispelled. On one occasion, Jesus described his followers as leaven in bread, and perhaps this is a more meaningful illustration. The church has always appeared to be weak. Indeed, for most of its history it has seemed to be dying. Yet it has moved within its world proclaiming justice, honesty, and decency and, in the end, making them prevail. Apparently, this is what Jesus expected of his followers and what he intended for them to do. On that faraway day, he gave them their instructions: "Go out and become the salt that flavors the world and the light that destroys the darkness." This is at least one meaning of our text.

The other day, in searching for the hidden implications of this passage, I saw another meaning which had not occurred to me before. Jesus was not only instructing his disciples in what they ought to do, but he was also stating a principle of life itself. He used two items in his illustrations

which were very familiar to his listeners. The first
was salt. The ancients built their ovens out-of-
doors, packing salt under the tiles to retain the
heat. After a while, the salt became contaminated,
so they dug it up, discarded it, and put new salt
in its place. This may be the picture here, but, in
any case, if salt no longer serves its purpose, it is
useless. The other example Jesus used was light.
The houses in Palestine were extremely dark. The
only lamp available was a vessel filled with oil,
floating a wick. Jesus asked, if you kindle a lamp
and cover it, of what value is it? From our vantage
point, the two analogies convey a common truth.
Whether you are speaking of salt or light, it must
fulfill its purpose or it is useless. Jesus, therefore,
was not so much telling us what we ought to do,
as revealing to us the way life is. I can think of at
least two reasons why this is true.

## II

First, if life is to have meaning, it must have a
purpose. The belief that we have a purpose in
life worthy of our allegiance can give us courage,
undergird us with strength, and enable us to
master life as nothing else can. At the same time,
nothing is more disastrous to a sense of well-being
than the knowledge that our lives are not going any-

where, and that what we are doing has no meaning.

Cecil Myers tells a story in his book *When Crisis Comes* about two men who were talking one day. One said to the other, "Do you ever take your wife gifts when you go home at night?" "Never have," said his friend. "Well, you ought to try it. It would make her appreciate you and love you more." So that night he stopped and bought her a dozen red roses, a box of candy, a book, some magazines, and a bottle of perfume. She met him at the door. He handed her the gifts, and she began to cry. "What's the matter with you?" he asked. "Here I bring you all these nice presents, and you stand there crying like a baby!" "This has been the worst day I ever lived," his wife said. "This morning about ten o'clock the water heater burst. At noon the cook got mad and quit, and now you come home drunk!" In a rough sort of way this may illustrate my point. Life is always bad when you work hard and what you do seems to have no meaning.

Jesus said this same thing a long time ago. If salt serves no purpose, it is useless. We are grappling now with manifestations of this problem. Industry, for example, is sensing its implications. A man who turns a bolt or clamps a wire in place with no idea of the end results may well become a psychological problem for his employer. Hence there is an ever-increasing effort on the part of industry to motivate employees by consultation, rather than by authoritative direction. We also see this as one of the problems afflicting our nation. At one time Americans carried a dream of destiny. Somewhere along the way the dream has become tarnished and marred. We are beginning to lose our sense of national purpose. As a consequence, we are being torn apart by internal disorder. We are no longer sure of what we are protesting against and demonstrating for. The church is suffering a similar predicament. We are not sure whether our mission is to preserve the institution or to become the servant church. We are thus divided among ourselves and, in many ways, are neutralizing our strength in internal wrangles. I suspect our malady is simply that we have lost the power of a purpose.

It has been said that creation does not easily tolerate uselessness. Nature tends to eliminate anything which serves no purpose. The dinosaur became a drag on the evolutionary process and thus ended in the graveyard. I cannot demonstrate the universal validity of this proposition; but it does seem to me that there is little use for salt that has lost its savor, or for lamps that will not burn. I would be surprised if the same principle is not equally valid anywhere in life.

## III

The other truth which seems apparent in this lesson is that life's purpose must be constructive if life is to be meaningful. It is not doing violence to our text to read this meaning into it. Jesus said, "Let your light so shine that men may see your good works and glorify God." That is to say, let the purpose of your life be in harmony with the purposes of God.

Occasionally, I hear someone say that we should be happy in our work. I am never quite sure what this means. There is some work we have to do which is absolute drudgery, and there seems to be no good way to change this. All of us have some of this kind of work to do—even Methodist ministers. It is dull, unexciting, and agonizing. When we say we enjoy our work, we are speaking of the satisfaction we derive from doing something meaningful.

The mechanization and compartmentalizing of modern industry have sometimes made the possibility of a person's finding a meaningful vocation exceedingly difficult. Hence, there is a strong temptation to see one's work solely as a means of holding body and soul together. When one views his work only from this vantage point, he is almost always unhappy in it. Jesus, however, urges us to elevate the most common and routine task of life into something exciting and satisfying by remembering that we can serve God and our fellowman in whatever we do. This can be done in the carpenter's shop, in the kitchen, on the assembly line, or in the office as effectively as it can be done in the church, and sometimes even more so.

Carl Michalson, a professor at Drew University, died in a plane crash not too long ago. Before his death he wrote a book entitled, *Faith for Personal Crises.* I found helpful his contention that God does not always call men to specific vocations. He calls them to salvation. "It comes to you where you are. The priority, then, is not with the question as to what you should do, but with the question as to whether you will admit God into what you are doing." This means that the important thing in life is not that God has called us to our vocations, but that, in the vocations we have chosen, we do what God has called all Christians to do.

On that day long ago when Jesus sat talking with his people, he saw their dull and listless spirits. He watched them toil at their daily tasks, trying to hold body and soul together until death released them from their ceaseless strivings. He knew that life was intended to be more than aimless wandering and meaningless effort. "Now," he said, "let me tell you how it is. Your work must be more than simply a means of sustaining your life. It must be transformed into something consistent with the total purposes of God. Let your light so shine—wherever you are, in the shop, at the fishing boats, or even in the fields—that God's love will be evident to all men. Every once in a while, when I become weary of the same old task and the same dull routines that so easily beset my profession, this thought brings me up short. What I need to think about is not changing jobs, but finding ways and means of serving God in the job that I have. Now and then, when I manage to achieve this, life comes alive, and each day seems a special gift of God. Do you suppose this might work for all of us?

# Morality—The Way It Is

*Matthew 5:17-20*

In the Old Testament we read of some people who have often received unfair treatment in the sermonizing of the centuries. Their story appears in the eleventh chapter of Genesis and is known as the "Legend of the Tower of Babel." According to the tradition, a band of people wandered over the trackless wilderness of the ancient world, seeking food for their cattle and a place to grow their simple gardens. One day in their councils these primitive folk became concerned about the possibility of getting lost on the rugged terrain of their uncharted world. They conceived a daring plan to enable them to find direction no matter where they traveled. "Come," they said to one another, "and let us build a tower so high that its top will reach the heavens, lest we be scattered abroad over the face of the earth."

History has judged these people to be vain and proud in their architectural dreams. Perhaps there is sufficient evidence in the story to warrant this conclusion. However, I wonder if these ancient people were not akin to all mankind, sharing a compulsion common to all of us. The problem of finding direction in life has never been easy. Man has always dreamed of finding a tower from which he might obtain his bearings. The search has become acute in our time. *Newsweek* magazine, when commenting on the moral permissiveness of the latter sixties, made this observation: "More than ever we need direction from mature leaders who see the forward energies of their age clearly and can enter into a rational and life-enhancing social covenant with those who will inherit the society." The subtle implications of that comment from a nonreligious magazine indicate our kinship with those ancient dreamers who sought a tower for direction on the confusing landscape of their day.

Today we are caught up in a sharp controversy over morality. The argument has a slightly different dimension from that of other generations. Our fathers believed that they knew what was right even though they might not live by it. Our generation is concerned, however, not only with the problem of doing what is right, but in knowing what the right is. The towers by which we make our value judgments have become obscured. We are asking now the basic question: "Should we decide to live morally erect, can anyone tell us what morality is?"

The portion of the Sermon on the Mount that we have chosen to discuss here deals with this. The followers of Jesus apparently asked simple questions: "Master, how should we live—what is right?" Jesus did not evade their questions. Perhaps in the most pointed language of his ministry, he told them how it was. Before we consider his words, let us look at a couple of traditional positions on the questions, which have persisted through the centuries.

# I

The first is *legalism*. Written into the traditions of Israel was an old story about the exodus from Egypt. Hebrew slaves had escaped the bondage of Egyptian taskmasters. They were on their dangerous journey to the Promised Land. Somewhere out there in the wilderness, they began to ponder the necessity of a moral tower. One day Moses disappeared from camp. When he returned, he

brought two tables of stone, upon which were in-
scribed ten laws of life. The traditions of the
campfires held that Moses had received these laws
on Mount Sinai, and that they were written in
God's own hand. History has labeled these laws
the Ten Commandments. The Hebrews believed
them to be sacred absolutes in which God had
said his final word. The Hebrews said that the
Ten Commandments, in spite of their negative
character, constituted the divine definition of
morality.

Obviously, the Ten Commandments were general statements and needed to be applied to
specific situations. Hence, the Hebrews began to
make an effort to make explicit what was implicit
in them. William Barclay describes the results of
their efforts to reduce general principles to specific
rules. Consider the commandment on the Sabbath. One day in each week was to be kept holy
and on it no work was to be done. This was the
principle, but these ancient Jews were sticklers for
precise definition. They raised the question,
"What is work?" Surely work meant to carry a
burden, and so burden had to be defined. The
scribal law laid it down as "food equal to the
weight of a dried fig, enough wine for mixing in
a goblet, milk enough for one swallow, paper
enough to write a custom's notice upon, and

enough ink to write two letters," and so on. Not surprisingly, their definition raised more questions than it answered. Is it lawful to lift a lamp from one place to another, or for a man to carry his child on the Sabbath day? Was not healing working on the Sabbath? This, too, had to be spelled out. Clearly, some wounds, injuries, and illnesses had to receive care. The conclusion concerning this was interesting: A patient could be treated on the Sabbath sufficiently to keep him from getting worse, but nothing could be done to make him better. You could bandage a wound, but no ointment could be used.

From our vantage point, this hairsplitting definition of morality is absurd. However, let us remember that revised editions of it have lingered across the ages, and are still around. Puritanism is a case in point. For the most part, such a morality was based on negative restraints. In our own time, there are still manifestations of it. Can you remember debates on the morality of playing cards, wearing cosmetics, attending movies, and even of certain hair styles, etc.? Such a definition is a natural result when morality is approached negatively. Morality does involve "Thou shalt nots," but when negativism is carried to its ultimate extreme, it in itself becomes immoral. Jesus understood this. "When people," he said on one

57

occasion, "are allowed to starve or suffer in order to preserve the prohibition of working on the Sabbath, the moral law becomes a moral problem." Moral negativism is not enough.

## II

The second position is *anti-legalism*. Mack Stokes tells of a woman who said that she did not like the Ten Commandments because they put ideas in her head. This woman probably has a lot of sympathizers for various reasons. It was apparently evident, even to the Jews in Jesus' day, that negative legalism was impossible. How else can you explain the reason for Jesus' comment on the law? He saw that people were overwhelmed by thousands of requirements subdividing the Ten Commandments into minute particles. The burden was so heavy that it stifled life. People spent all their time trying to keep the law with no time to live. While this problem is not clearly described in our text, I think it is implied. The common people were in rebellion. It was humanly impossible to keep all the regulations implicit in the law; so they must have said, "Master, can't we abandon the law?"

It is characteristic of human nature to react against an extreme with an extreme. At least, there are many examples of this scattered through the records of man. The story of the Prodigal Son depicts a boy reacting against the discipline of the farm by seeking the absolute freedom of the far country. In our own day, this same kind of thing is happening. A new generation, in rebellion against the rules of another generation that may have been too restrictive, refuses to accept any restraint at all. Perhaps you saw a television drama that was broadcast a year or so ago. A young congressman, incensed over corruption in government, was willing to destroy the government itself in order to correct the corruption. Our newspapers have been filled with this kind of thing. The West Coast hippie riots are examples in point. These youngsters, in their rebellion against the unhealthy repression of natural human impulses, have overreacted into an unhealthy expression of those same impulses.

I read in the newspaper not long ago about a couple of young people who had once been deeply committed Christians, completely puritanical in their moral attitudes. "But we no longer believe that," one of them said. "Man was made to be free, not restricted by legalistic baggage." It seemed ironic to me that this confession was made in a police station, where the two were in custody charged with a chain of robberies stretching from coast to coast. They were learning what man periodically discovers: Negative legalism is not the way to life, but anti-legalism is just as unrealistic.

## III

Against these two positions, Jesus took his stand. Look for a moment at what he said.

First, Jesus insisted that the principle of the law is valid. "I came," he said, "not to destroy the law. Heaven and earth will pass away before one jot or tittle of the law is lost." The Commandments stand, simply because they conform to the way God made his world. They are descriptive of the way things were intended to work. There is built into creation a cycle of rest and work, the sanctity of the home, the necessity of truthfulness, the sacredness of property rights, the destructiveness of envy, the value of human life. Violate these basic principles and you are in conflict with circumstances that are intended to prevail. This is simply the way things are, and to try to repeal these principles is as foolish as attempting to repeal the law of gravity. "Hold to these principles," said Jesus, "and teach your children to do so."

In addition, Jesus went beyond this statement to a concept which his day never fully comprehended, and which we still have trouble understanding. The law is made for man and not against him. It is a manifestation of God's love for man, and man's application of the law must be made with this in mind. This concept of the law has deep philosophical and theological implications that most of us may never fully understand. We can, however, observe some practical implications of it which are apparent in the life of Jesus.

Take the principle of the Sabbath, for instance. For the Jews, it must have been a day of dread. We can understand why. I remember from my boyhood certain "saints," who seemed to imply that there was something solemn and sad about Sunday. They instructed me to walk quietly and to speak softly; on other occasions, they talked about "making a joyful noise unto the Lord." I sensed something inconsistent in what they said. Jesus put this whole matter into a new perspective. "The law of the Sabbath," he said, "is subject to a higher law—the law of love. And whatever love requires you to do, you must do, even on the Sabbath."

This, I think, is the tower that men who travel over the confused moral terrain of our day need to see. The law of love is supreme. It does not negate the Ten Commandments. Rather, it undergirds them and transforms them from negative legalism into positive principles of action. When

61

we seek to translate these general principles into specific application, we must ask the question, "What does love require?"

A long time ago, Augustine said, "Love God, and do as you please." It would be easy to conclude that this principle is too liberal—and perhaps it is. Nevertheless, if our lives were committed into the hands of a jury, and to sit on that jury we could choose between those who knew the law and those who had sensed and acknowledged the love of God, we would choose the latter. On occasions they might violate the letter of the law, but they would keep its spirit. Historically, the people who love God have used the law to enrich rather than to impoverish mankind.

We stand today amid a world of problems ranging all the way from interpersonal relationships to international turmoil. Against these problems of incredible complexity, mankind is seeking right solutions—some principles from which we may take direction. As we seek an answer, there comes to us a voice from a long-ago day and a faraway place asking, "What does love require?" The word of Jesus is not only a word of instruction, but also a word of challenge. What do you suppose might happen to our world, personally and collectively, if from this time and in this place we were to accept his challenge? Suppose we asked honestly, not what economics, custom, or the law requires, but what love requires? Jesus indicated that a world of darkness would be transformed into a world of light. Do you suppose he was right?

# Survival—The Way It Is

*Matthew 5:38-42*

A national television network made a study of the causes of the restlessness of our generation. Reporters were dispatched across the country to talk with people of every age and in almost every circumstance. The editors attempted to analyze their findings and reduce to a few basic principles the underlying causes of the seething ferment afflicting our times. One of their conclusions was particularly interesting. It said, in effect, that modern man is suffering from a subconscious fear of danger. It is a fear that is not openly discussed very much. It is rather an inarticulate, vague uneasiness that has filtered down through the conscious mind into the subconscious. It is an ominous fear deep inside contemporary man that he may not survive.

The causes of this uneasiness are many. There is, of course, the presence of *the bomb*. There is not much evidence that the threat of nuclear disaster is the paramount concern of most people. Few of us seem to believe that premeditated atomic warfare is a possibility. There are those who believe that some irresponsible person may accidentally trigger global catastrophe. The major causes of our anxiety are more subtle and less obvious. The violence of riots, the festering frustration of deprived people, the dangerous disregard of law and order, and the irresponsibility of great segments of our society are seen as potential hazards to the security of everyone. The average American seems concerned about his own safety and that of his family in a world that is filled with conflict and hostility.

It is rather strange, is it not, that a people who have devised so many things to enrich life have been unable to devise some way to live it without fear of losing it? After all, it doesn't matter how much you have to enjoy if you are not around to enjoy it. If a mother has to worry about her child making it home from school without becoming the victim of hatred and violence, or a father must live in constant fear that his family is in danger, life cannot be very meaningful. Such anxieties are getting to us, and we are beginning now to ask ourselves, "Does our world have to be this way?" Is it not possible for man—even in these confusing times—to find the key to survival?

Long ago, Jesus, in the Sermon on the Mount, made two or three interesting observations: "If a man strikes you on one cheek, turn the other. If he compels you to go one mile, go with him two. If he takes your coat, give him your cloak also." How unusual and unnatural these words appear to be. How unlikely they seem as a blueprint to survival, but do you suppose that they hold the answer for us? What is Jesus saying here that may help us ease the hostilities in our world and enable us to live at peace?

## I

First, Jesus is saying that survival is dependent upon unity. The day in which these statements were made was one of Roman domination over the land of the Jews. The Jews have never lived in bondage gracefully, and the arrogant Roman legions particularly inflamed them. There was strong animosity toward the invading soldiers, resulting in a deep resentment that burned in the hearts of the Jews. This resentment could have been the reason for Jesus' comment. Perhaps the Jews said to him, "Master, how can we rid our-

SURVIVAL—THE WAY IT IS

selves of these evil oppressors?" Jesus must have answered them, "I can tell you this. The old law of an eye for an eye will never work. This only sets off a chain reaction of hatred which will end in disintegration. Somehow divided people must get together. Let me suggest a new direction. If a Roman soldier compels you to go with him one mile, go with him two."

This principle of unity seems consistent with everything that we know about creation. Nature is committed to the preservation of it. *Life* magazine carried a comment made by Frank Borman upon his return from the orbital flight around the moon. "We are one hunk of ground, water, air, clouds, floating around in space. From out there it really is 'one world.'" I doubt that you need a lunar observation post to determine this. Even a casual observation of the physical world will give evidence of it. Nature does not easily tolerate disunity. Every particle of matter from the atom to the stars is blended into a total plan. To make any attempt to upset this unity is to invite disaster. Togetherness—a word often used in a different context—is really an accurate description of the way things are.

It is only reasonable to expect that this principle prevails even in the world of human relationships. Here, as in nature, unity is the key that unlocks

67

the doorway to survival. Individuals estranged from each other are never safe from danger. A home divided against itself will not stand. No marriage can endure when partners work at odds with each other. A community splintered into opposing factions is the breeding ground for riots, strife, and violence. And what is true here must be true in the world community. Unity among men appears to be the intended plan of creation. Every known violation of this principle has produced a bitter harvest.

The oldest living things on this planet are said to be the giant Sequoia trees. E. Stanley Jones lists six reasons for their survival, among them, the fact that the trees always grow in clumps or clusters. Their roots intertwine and in the time of storm they give support to each other—survival by mutual dependence. Has man ever devised any other way to weather the storms of the centuries? Somewhere people who intend to live together have to get together. History is finally bringing us to the place where there is no other alternative.

## II

Second, Jesus is telling us that unity can be achieved only through love. There are really only two ways to approach this matter of unity. One is by force. The trouble with trying to achieve unity by force, however, is that the result is always temporary and superficial as long as force is the only factor involved. This is not to say that force is unnecessary. External pressure is always necessary to maintain order, but it is not the final answer as you and I well know. Even Napoleon recognized this. "Caesar, Charlemagne, and I," he said, "built our empires on power and they have perished. Jesus founded his on love and it remains."

"The only hope of lasting unity," said Jesus, "is love." Love alone can break the cycle of hate and bring forth the best in human nature. A man and his wife had had a quarrel about something unimportant. The next morning as the husband was leaving for work, he noticed a button missing from his shirt. "Will you sew this button on?" he asked. "Yes," she said, still remembering the quarrel. "But why do you always ask me to do this kind of thing at inconvenient times?" Nevertheless, she sewed it on, and as he was leaving she said, "I need ten dollars extra for some things I want this month." The man growled, "I only have five. What do you do with your money anyway?" All day long the woman reflected on this event, conscience-stricken over their quarrel. Finally, she decided to stop the argument. Going to the dresser where he kept his shirts, she found the one he would wear the next day. Picking up her scissors, she clipped a button off and went her way. The next morning her husband growled again, "Will you sew this button on?" "I'll be glad to," she said. "Let me get my needle. It's a joy to do something for you." She sewed it on and hugged him tenderly. "By the way, I need a little money for household expenses. I know how hard you work for what we have. If you don't have it, perhaps we can get by." "Oh," he said, "here's ten; no, make it twenty. I just don't see how you manage to get by on so little."

Now I am well aware that this little story may illustrate a perversion of the Christian concept of love, but it is not without its point. Attitudes usually provoke similar responses. Hate generally produces hate, and love has a way of breeding love. Just how far can this principle be carried? No one really knows. That it works on the level of simple human relationships is generally accepted. A lot of us wonder if we can depend upon it in the larger problems of hostility.

Something happened several years ago that makes me feel that this principle does have wider implications. I was serving on the board of one of our church colleges, and a nasty dispute arose over a rule in the college handbook. I was asked to chair a committee to bring about a solution.

I faced the task with great anxiety. The students were adamant in their position. They did not like the rule and they intended to change it. Finally, in desperation, we asked the students if any rule on the matter were needed. "Of course," they replied. "Well," we suggested, "you write the rule, one that you believe to be honest and just and right, and we will do our best to live by it." They worked for two weeks, strictly on their honor, and finally sent the committee the rule they had written. To our surprise their rule was stiffer and more exacting than our own.

I am not suggesting that students run colleges, or that this principle works with the precision of a law in physics. Nevertheless, it is true that the *gospel of the second mile* puts the offender on the spot. If there is anything good inside him, it will show. If kindness beyond the call of duty does not effect reconciliation and unity, it is a sure bet that nothing will.

## III

Finally, Jesus is reminding us that the search for unity is an active pursuit. Once I saw a comment made by Will Rogers. Back during World War I when German submarines were mutilating Allied shipping, he proposed getting rid of the

U-boats by heating the ocean to 212 degrees. Then as the boats surfaced, battleships could pick them off. Someone asked him how he intended to heat the ocean. "That's a detail," he quipped, "and I don't deal in details. I only establish policy." Could this be one of the reasons we are in such grave difficulty today? All of us deal in policy, and no one gives attention to the details.

In the Beatitudes, Jesus said, "Blessed are the peacemakers, for they shall be called the sons of God." The word peacemaker is an active word implying more than wistful thinking. Desiring unity is an admirable virtue, but it hardly accomplishes the task. The desperate need is not so much for those who want peace, but for those who will make peace. It is not just a matter of stating policy. Someone must work at the details.

You can see this idea clearly focused in our text today. Imagine the faces of those people when Jesus looked them squarely in the eye and said, "You want peace and unity in your world. That is a commendable dream, but it is not enough. Harmony among men requires action from someone. If a man strikes you on one cheek, turn the other. If he compels you to go one mile, go two. There can be no unity without a commitment to action."

During the next few years, The United Methodist Church will be attempting to enlist people throughout its membership in a ministry of reconciliation. We as churchmen are being asked to come down from the policy level and go out among the estranged peoples of this country and world and work with details. It is dirty work and not any of it is easy. We must try to confront the lonely, the diseased, the sinful, the confused, and the lost people all around us and tell them of God's concern for them. Since the day when this call was issued by the church, I have been trying to find a way to excuse myself, but I keep running into these words of our Master: "I say into you, if a man strikes you on one cheek, turn the other; if he compels you to go one mile, go with him two. If he takes your coat, give him your cloak also. Come down from your policy-making and get to work on the details." Somehow I get the strange feeling that Jesus was speaking directly to you and me!

# Love—The Way It Is

*Matthew 5:43-48*

I hope that you have seen a little book written a few years ago by Carl Burke entitled *God Is for Real, Man.* If you have read it, you will remember that it contains a series of biblical passages interpreted in the language of the street. Burke describes it as the Bible translated by "bad-tempered angels with busted halos." In many ways, it is a unique and startling translation. Noah is referred to as a "cool cat"; the story of the Prodigal Son is labeled "Throwin' a Party for Junior"; and the feeding of the five thousand is described as "Some Lunch, Huh?"

There is a place for this kind of thing. If nothing else, it puts a lot of timeworn ideas in a fresh and interesting light. One of the problems with the traditional language of religion is that it has a way of becoming encrusted with unintended meanings. Once in a while, we need to take the central ideas of our faith, shake the dust from them, and reconsider their original connotations.

One idea that is forever falling among bad companions is the Christian doctrine of love. It started out having one meaning, but, as language grows and word concepts change, we keep losing that meaning in linguistic difficulties. Persistent efforts have been made to correct this. At times we have attempted new words. When the King James Version of the Bible was authorized in 1611, its translators, following the lead of John Wycliffe and others, used the word *charity*. However, the common usage of charity did not convey the exact idea. Subsequent versions have almost always returned to the use of the word *love*. Apparently, we are going to have to be content with this. The English language seems to provide no suitable substitute. We are confronted, therefore, with the constant necessity of defining the limits of love as used in a Christian context.

The heart of the Sermon on the Mount deals with a particular definition of love. Unless we understand this, much of the sermon is unintelligible. Although the answer may already be clear to most of us, I want to ask the question again,

"What does the word *love* mean as the Christian uses it?"

## I

We might well begin with a consideration of the word itself. In this study of the Sermon on the Mount, I have attempted a thesis which I believe is credible. These first few chapters of Matthew's gospel constitute a description, not of what life ought to be, but of what it must be. The passage seems to be in conflict with this thesis. Jesus said, "Love your enemies." Few commandments seem so utterly impossible. Love, as we usually understand it, is an attitude of the heart anchored in the emotions. On this basis, we wonder if Jesus was really making sense. Can you issue orders to your heart and command affection for someone whom you despise? Nothing seems more unnatural and out of keeping with our natures.

C. S. Lewis did a great deal to make the Christian faith understandable to the people of the latter half of the twentieth century. Writing on this very theme in *Mere Christianity*, he made an interesting comment. "Love, in the Christian sense, does not mean an emotion. It is a state not of the feelings but of the will." Here is something that needs to be pointed out to those of us who because of language limitations must read the Bible in English. We have only the one word—*love*—to describe several ideas, whereas not all languages suffer this limitation.

William Barclay reminds us that the Greeks, for example, had several words for love, among them one that speaks of *family love*. This is the kind of natural affection which we have for our kin. Parents do not have to be taught to love their children, or children their parents. We have an almost instinctive feeling of warmth for our kinsmen.

The Greeks also had another word to describe the feeling that a man has for a woman, or a woman for a man. This is *romantic love* and most often, in our day, is associated with sex. This, too, is a sort of intuitive affection which was created into the nature of man.

There is still another Greek word that describes what we usually mean by *close friendships*. Two people are attracted to each other by a warmth of fellowship. They share a mutual affection for each other. They confide in one another, pouring out the deepest secrets of their hearts. They have similar interests, attracting personalities, and kindred spirits.

These kinds of love are anchored largely in the affections. They are natural to human nature and require little effort. A normal mother does not need to be instructed to love her child; opposite sexes fall in love with each other in the normal scheme of things; and friendship is a natural arrangement in human affairs. However, Jesus is telling us to love our enemies, those to whom we are not attracted, people who do not respond to our friendship—people whom we do not like. How can we love people for whom we have no affection? Can we order our hearts to love those for whom, by nature, we have no feeling? Apparently, Jesus is referring to a particular kind of love, which is slightly different in character from the other three. It is here that C. S. Lewis' insight has been helpful. Christian love is not so much a matter of the emotions as of the will.

## II

What did Jesus mean when he said, "Love your enemies"? Roger Lovette, in the February 1969 edition of *Pulpit Digest*, reminds us of Frederick Speakman's story about a minister who had a troublemaker in his congregation. The man was born in the "objective" mood and never got over it. He considered it his divine calling to lead the opposition no matter which direction the church decided to go. One day the minister, particularly disturbed by the man, reminded a friend that Jesus said we should love our enemies, but "how can we, as Christians, love a man like that!" The friend replied pointedly, "Christian love is not fondness. It is not how you feel. It is *what you do!*"

Does this not grasp the meaning of what Jesus is saying in our text? No matter how we feel toward our fellowman—whether we are naturally attracted to him or not—we are under obligation as Christians to approach him in goodwill, seeking his best interest even as we seek our own. Think for a moment about the Golden Rule. Jesus did not say, "*Feel* about others as you feel about yourself." Rather, he said, "*Do* unto others as you would have them do unto you." The verb here is one of action, involving conscious effort rather than natural inclination.

Will Rogers is quoted as having said that he never met a man he didn't like. While I admire his spirit, I must confess that I have met some people that I have liked a lot less than others. I have also earnestly attempted to like these unlovable people, but I have never quite managed to make my heart listen to my head. But like them or not, I am not released from my obligation to approach these people in goodwill, seeking their best interest, ignoring their unlovable natures. No matter what their response, I must not deviate from that approach.

This is the kind of love that Jesus is requiring of us in the Sermon on the Mount. Our natural inclination is to respond only to those for whom we have warm affection or feeling. Jesus, however, inserts a new dimension into this usual concept of love. Christian love is not a feeling but an act of will. It is true that when we approach unlovable people in goodwill, we usually feel compassion for them. But even if we do not like our enemies, we have the obligation to love them. This is the clear admonition of the Sermon on the Mount.

## III

Of course, the question remains, "Why does life demand that we love our enemies?" Why not exchange goodwill with those who express goodwill toward us? We of all people should understand this when we reflect on the experiences of our world across the past fifty years. My father used to tell a story from his pulpit about a man who invited some friends to his home for a weekend. After the usual introductions, the guests gathered in small groups, some to talk, some to play games on the lawn, and others simply to roam about their host's estate. Sometime during the visit, one of the guests decided to take over the place. He attracted some followers by promising to divide the conquered estate with them. Soon the spirit of rebellion swept through the house, and the animosity erupted into violence. One group barricaded itself inside the house. The other group, enraged by the despicable behavior of the rebels, set fire to it. The story ended with the estate in ruins and the guests empty-handed.

This story never really happened, but some of us are wondering if it might not occur. I have heard recently of people roaming the streets shouting, "Burn, baby, burn." It seems to me that other people may be barricaded inside the buildings being threatened by fire, determined not to give an inch and to hold at any cost. But history is beginning to teach us a bitter lesson. The stand-patters are not going to be able to hold the house, and the revolutionaries can only burn it down. Nobody can win. Unless someone on one side or the other is willing to ignore feelings, rise above affection, and act in love toward the unlovable, the house will end in shambles. The irony of it all is that the house does not belong to any of us at all. It is the Heavenly Father's house and we are only his guests.

Many maintain that the day of the old swap-out —where we love only those who love us—is gone.

## THERE'S NO OTHER WAY

The truth is that it has been gone a long, long time, and we are just beginning to find it out. The day of reconciliation is here, not because this is the way it ought to be, but because this is the way it must be. We must find a way to bridge the gap between generations, nations, races, social and economic groups. Jesus said, "Love your enemies"—not because he required it, but because life demands it. That's the way it is; there's no other way!

# Investment—The Way It Is

*Matthew 6:19-21*

Several years ago, William Stidger published a series of books under the general title, *There Are Sermons in Stories*. In the first of those books he relates an incident which occurred at a construction site near Providence, Rhode Island. The steel framework of a large building was being erected. One morning, as the author passed, he discovered that a workman had fallen. The foreman explained what had happened. A stiff but erratic wind had been blowing in from the coast that morning. One of the men, new on the job, was standing on a girder, leaning against a strong gust. The wind suddenly shifted, and, before the man could recover his balance, he was gone.

The point of this little story came back to me

again the other day as I was rereading the Sermon on the Mount. One of the things that must have concerned Jesus most about his followers was the chronic temptation apparent among them to trust the uncertain and to lean on the unreliable. He had a clear insight into what man is seeking. The basic dream of the human heart has always been for an abundant and meaningful life. Jesus had no quarrel with this. He knew that we were entitled to such a life by the charter of creation. Our problem is not in our goal, but in the manner we attempt to achieve it.

It must have been this concern that prompted Jesus to set down for us the words of our text. "Lay not up for yourselves treasures on earth, where moth and rust corrupt and where thieves break through and steal, but lay up for yourselves treasures in heaven, where neither moth nor rust corrupts and where thieves do not break through and steal." The traditional interpretation of this passage would lead us to believe that Jesus is directing us to give attention to the next world with no concern for this one. It may be, however, that this text has a "this-world" focus, which we ignore only at great peril.

Inherent in the basic message of this passage is the reminder that life is a matter of constant investment. Somewhere I saw an account of a missionary who was traveling with a native to one of the outposts of his assignment. The land had a long history of cannibalism. The missionaries had worked diligently to change this and felt that they had succeeded. As the two men were climbing a rather steep trail, still far from their destination, it came time for lunch. The native opened his lunch box and began to eat seriously and with full deliberation. The missionary was impatient and prodded the man to hurry, but the man refused to be hurried. When asked to explain his behavior, the native replied, "I will not hurry. I am eating my wife." The missionary was horrified. Had the labors of the church been completely in vain? Then the native went on to explain, in a beautiful way, that the missionary had misunderstood. What he meant was that his wife had used a part of her life in the preparation of his lunch. She had invested herself as she had given her time. He was under obligation to treat her investment as a sacred sacrifice.

Sometimes we let this rather solemn thought slip out of our minds in the feverish activity of our lives. Often we talk about saving life, but, in a real sense, we never do. Life is constantly moving between the limits of birth and death. We are compelled by the scheme of creation to use it in one way or another. This is not a matter of choice. Consciously or unconsciously our lives are being used up. That seems to be the way it is.

Of course, inherent in this whole process is the fact that the use of every moment of life becomes a determining factor in the nature of every succeeding moment. This is the unspoken implication in our text that we sometimes forget. Jesus did not offer us three alternatives in laying up our treasures. He did not suggest that we could refrain from laying up any treasures at all. He could not say this, of course, because of the nature of life itself. We are always laying up treasures, consciously or unconsciously. Perhaps we do not intend it, but every moment of life is a moment of investment.

Every study of human personality gives evidence of this, does it not? What we have thought or done at any given time is not isolated to itself, but has bearing on every other thought or deed for the rest of our lives. Not one of us is able to chop time into little pieces, throwing away what we do not like and keeping what we choose. We would like it this way, but creation does not grant us this privilege. Life counts the conscious as well as the unconscious decisions, and what you have at any given time is largely the sum total of what has passed. Jesus could not say to us, "Cease making your investment." He had to tell it the way it is.

## INVESTMENT—THE WAY IT IS

"You *have* to lay up your treasures. You cannot stop that. The only choice you have is in the manner in which your investment is made." There are really only two alternatives.

## I

This text first comments on the nature of earthly treasures. There is a minister in New York who has written some graphic descriptions on his observations of drug addiction. His book, which is being studied by many thoughtful people nowadays, contains one theme. There is a law of diminishing returns that operates when life is invested in this direction. Drugs which have initial potency become increasingly less effective with continued use.[1]

Dig a bit into what Jesus is saying here. In his day a man's wealth was often measured by the extent of his wardrobe. Biblical writers often refer to robes of purple as the symbol of riches. Status was established by the number of garments one possessed. At times articles of clothing became coveted treasures in the marketplace. "Now," said Jesus, "don't set your heart on these things. They are subject to the laws of diminishing returns. At

[1] David Wilkerson, *Hey, Preach: You're Comin' Through!* (Westwood, N. J.: Fleming H. Revell, 1968).

first they are valuable, but the moths can get to them and destroy them. You are foolish to build your happiness on things you can lose."

The folly of trying to build happiness on things you can lose! Contrary to an all-too-common interpretation, this thought is not a prohibition on the acquisition of possessions. Rather, it is a commentary on the use of them—on the place that they take in our lives. Shortly after graduating from college I bought a new car. I had three years of Divinity School ahead which had to be worked out penny by penny. But it was a magnificent automobile—four on the column, twin-barrel carburetor, and chrome in the right places. I took it by to show to my father. He came out to look it over. He walked around it and quietly asked, "How many payments?" I told him. "Have you found a job yet?" "No," I replied. Then in his quiet but penetrating wisdom he remarked, "Son, you don't own a car. It owns you." And he was right. Every day the chrome of that car glittered less. Happiness built on something I could not keep—I will be a long time forgetting that. Burns once wrote something about this in his poem "Tam o' Shanter":

> But pleasures are like poppies spread,
> You seize the flow'r, its bloom is shed!
> Or like the snow-falls in the river,
> A moment white—then melts for ever.

All that Jesus is doing in this little passage is reminding us that when life is invested in the pursuit of possessions, for the sake of possessions themselves, we are leaning on the wind. One day the wind will stop, and everything will be lost. When we examine all that we know about life— the sum total of human experience—wasn't Jesus telling it like it is? What man anywhere has ever found meaningful life in simply accumulating *things*? The momentary exhilaration is soon lost, the chrome fades, the moths have their picnic, or the wind shifts. Build your happiness on the possession of things and your peace will always be marred by the threat of loss and the anxiety of being left empty-handed.

## II

"But," said Jesus, "life can be invested in heavenly treasures." When Wallace Hamilton came with his sister to this country from Canada, they landed in Chicago. Their only money was Canadian. Hamilton had heard that the smart taxi drivers would take country people ten miles around the city on a two-block trip and then charge them accordingly. So Hamilton and his sister decided to take a streetcar. They lugged their baggage aboard and handed the driver a Canadian

THERE'S NO OTHER WAY

quarter. He handed it back, saying gruffly, "Counterfeit." They scrambled off in anger and carried their bags twenty blocks. The next day they exchanged their currency for money acceptable in the new country.[2]

Jesus' word to us is illustrated in Hamilton's story. The possessions of life can be exchanged—perishable treasures for eternal treasures. It is all a matter of the method of investment. Put what you have to the proper use, and the returns will bring increasing satisfaction.

On April 15, 1912, the White Star liner *Titanic* went down 1,600 miles northeast of New York City. One man who was a passenger on that tragic voyage was Robert J. Bateman. Bateman was a sort of diamond-in-the-rough evangelist. When it became apparent that there were not enough lifeboats for the 2,200 passengers aboard the ill-fated ship, some of the men stepped back to let the women and children have them. Bateman was one of those who gave their lives that night in the North Atlantic. As the ship went down, he led those left on board in the singing of a hymn. Most of the accomplishments of his lifetime went down with him. Bateman did one thing though that did not perish beneath the icy waters that evening. He

[2] J. Wallace Hamilton, *Ride the Wild Horses* (Westwood, N. J.: Fleming H. Revell, 1952), p. 63.

90

touched the life of a young man, who is now well in his eighties, and directed him to God. This man has probably done as much as any human being in modern times to create Christian goodwill across the world. His books have sold more than three and one-half million copies, and have been translated into eighteen languages. Stanley Jones, in his autobiography, *A Song of Ascents,* expressed his gratitude to Robert J. Bateman, who brought to him the richest treasure of his life.

No single illustration proves any rule. However, when I look back on my own life and everything that I have been able to learn from experience, the only real and abiding satisfactions I have had are those gained from using what I had to enrich the lives of others. Jesus was not making an idle promise when he suggested that if we want heavenly lives here or hereafter, we must use what we have in heavenly ways. It is simply a matter of making the right investments. It is the giving of what we have, and are, in the service of others. Life lived any other way is "leaning on the wind!"

# Worry—The Way It Is

*Matthew 6:25-33*

About twenty years ago an opinion poll was taken in Great Britain to determine the underlying fears troubling the British people. One of the interesting discoveries in that survey was that twenty-four out of twenty-five people were suffering from an abnormal and unhealthy anxiety. One person out of every ten was afraid of the dark; one in four was fearful of animals, mostly small ones; four out of five had fears of other people. One-fourth the persons interviewed expressed feelings of claustrophobia or related fears. The poll revealed that most of the fears were intensely personal and downright silly when seen by anyone but the persons themselves.

What would such an experiment uncover if

taken now—twenty years later? I suspect that the specific problems might have changed. We are better adjusted to some of these fears than preceding generations. Widespread air travel and life among the skyscrapers have in some ways diminished our fear of heights; the crowded condition of urbanized living has perhaps affected our feeling about life in closed places. It would seem reasonable to believe that the precise objects of our fears may have changed a bit, but the problem of fear is still among us, often with devastating consequences.

A college dean recently set in focus one aspect of this increasingly troublesome problem. There is growing emotional difficulty among young people. Youth, formerly regarded as the carefree and lighthearted stage of life, no longer appears to be that way. Many young people are suffering from deep and acute anxiety. One problem is the race for college. Youngsters are being driven by the notion that the failure to pass college entrance exams is total disaster and will result in social rejection. They are caught up in the mad competition of grades for the sake of grades. School is no longer an exciting adventure in learning, but a time for sleepless nights and anxious days. Add to this the pressurized nature of modern life, the depersonalization of society, and the threat of glob-

93

al disaster, and this generation has become a generation with a troubled mind.

It goes without saying that fear is not confined to youth. It is widespread across every age and segment of our society—as it probably has been in every generation. Apparently, this was true in the days of Jesus and accounts for what he said in this particular portion of the Sermon on the Mount. He saw his friends living on the edge of desperation, distracted by abnormal and destructive fears. One day he said to them, "Let's talk about this for a while. Let me explain to you some things about this whole matter of fear that you don't understand. Don't worry about your life. There is really no point in worrying." And so he began, "Consider the lilies of the field. . . ." For a long time now, men have read these words and found meaning in them. Perhaps we can find them helpful, too.

## I

We must begin by trying to understand exactly what Jesus was saying. In my recent study of the Sermon on the Mount, I have attempted to do something that I have never done seriously before. I have been looking closely at the words, seeking original meanings I had missed in years gone by.

I have discovered some interesting things that were not clear in the translations I have been using.

Consider the first phrase in this passage, for instance. In the King James Version it reads, "Take no thought for the morrow." One commentary suggests that this was perhaps the first attempt to translate what Jesus said in this manner. Wycliffe had it: "Be not busy to your life." Tyndale and the Geneva Bible put it this way: "Be not careful for your life." By the word careful they meant what it literally means, "full of care." If these older translations are correct, then the entire passage acquires a new meaning. Jesus is not advocating imprudent foresight, a shiftless, reckless, and thoughtless existence. He is, rather, condemning a worried, anxious fear that robs us of the joy of life.

This insight has been valuable to me. The impression that Christians are careless lotus-eaters, and that concern about life is unchristian is clearly in error. In our natures, the capacity to be afraid is a God-given one. Without it man probably would not cope with many of the dangers of his environment. It is man's fear of disease that drives him to conquer it; his concern about the terror of war that forces him to strive for peace; his fear of power that teaches him the necessity of controlling it. Such fear is neither unhealthy nor unchristian, anymore than is a child's fear of the fire.

I think that what Jesus is saying here is entirely different in principle. "Do not allow your concern for the eventualities of life to rob you of the meaning and significance of the present." Here is a word of wisdom. It is possible to become so preoccupied with the mistakes of the past, and the grim possibilities of the future, that we are rendered ineffective for the tasks at hand. That is the way a lot of us live.

Two illustrations help to clarify this: one of them trivial; the other more serious. Public speaking comes hard for me. The pressure of a weekly deadline has never lessened even after twenty years in this spot. The fear of coming to the worship hour on Sunday morning unprepared to do your best can rob you of your effectiveness in other duties. You find yourself living uptight all week, concentrating on the fear of tomorrow and missing the joys of today. This is one sin to which I must plead guilty far more often than I care to admit.

The same thing can happen in other ways. The other day a friend remarked to me that he had grown up during the days of the Great Depression, and it frightened him to think of the impression it had made on him. "Things were bad back there," he said, "inadequate food, meager clothing, never enough of anything. I was determined to improve my lot. I began to scrimp and save, to gather everything I could to be ready for any eventuality. I set a direction to my life which has almost become habitual. I find it difficult to enjoy anything without feeling guilty, to share my good fortune with others without doing it grudgingly, or to live pleasantly today without thinking about making enough for tomorrow." This, I think, is what Jesus is talking about. We call it worry. Jesus said it was foolishness.

## II

Why did Jesus say that worry is folly? For one thing, it is unnecessary. "Who among you," Jesus asks, "can add one cubit to his stature by worrying about it?" Isn't that telling it like it is? The lines in the drama of life are written in indelible ink, and anxiety provides no eraser.

For many years Alcoholics Anonymous has printed a little card which has been distributed across the world. Every once in a while, I pick it up and read it again. It goes something like this: "There are two days in every week about which we should not worry. One of these days is *yesterday* with its mistakes and cares, its faults and blunders.

97

All the money in the world cannot bring back *yesterday*. *Yesterday* is gone.

"The other day is *tomorrow* with its possible adversaries, its burdens, its large promise. *Tomorrow* is also beyond our immediate control. *Tomorrow's* sun will rise, either in splendor or behind a mask of clouds—but it will rise. Until it does, we have no stake in *tomorrow*, for it is as yet unborn.

"This leaves only one day—*today*. Any man can fight the battles of just one day. It is only when you and I add the burdens of those two awful eternities—*yesterday and tomorrow*—that we break down."

In some ways, this is a dangerous approach to life. Our days are connected, and the past and present always have bearing on the future. However, worry won't undo the past, or do much to change the future. It can only make today miserable.

## III

Worry is foolish also because it results in limited and distorted vision. Said Jesus, "Consider the lilies of the field and the birds of the air. God takes care of them." Essentially, worry is preoccupation with self. Its focus of attention is inward. Jesus is saying, "Look around you. God cares for the birds, the grass, the flowers. Are you not worth more than they?"

Our generation is very much *turned off* on any notion of the providence of God. This may be exactly the reason why we are so troubled. Anyone who for a single moment takes his eyes off himself and looks around will discover that no man completely controls himself and his destiny. Man is subject to an overriding hand committed to man's ultimate good. Evil has never dealt the final hand anywhere. If you care to look for it, you can find proof of this written on every page of history and in every experience of life.

## IV

The folly of worry! We are willing to accept the foolishness of worry, but we still find it difficult to live without anxiety? Jesus suggests an answer here. "Seek ye first the kingdom of God and his righteousness."

One of the greatest sermons of all times was preached many years ago by a man named Thomas Chalmers. The title of it was "The Expulsive Power of a Great Affection." The principle upon which that sermon rests is simply this: Two kings cannot occupy the same throne. Inevitably, one of them will depose the other. I suspect that this principle prevails throughout life. Fear and anxiety can be removed from our hearts only by the admission of another king.

Perhaps the most futile advice we can give ourselves in this whole matter is to say, "Do not worry." Nature does not easily tolerate a vacuum, especially in the human mind. One disposes of worry by giving his energies to something else. Jesus was fully aware of this that day as he addressed his people.

B. D. Napier, in his book *Prophets in Perspective*, tells a story about a little girl who approached a librarian and asked for a book on penguins. The book was found (a big one) and she went eagerly home with it. The next morning she was waiting to return the book when the library opened. "I wanted to learn something about penguins," she said sadly, "but not this much." There is something commendable about her reasoning. There is no sense in wasting time and energy on something that doesn't count. Jesus is saying to us that in order to rid ourselves of fear and anxiety we must give ourselves to something constructive.

Dean Inge used to say that the happy people are those who are producing something, and that we sometimes deceive ourselves by believing that a rest cure is the answer to our anxiety. In nine out of ten cases what we need is a work cure. In the Sermon on the Mount, Jesus said it another way: "Conform to the will of God; put a new king on the throne, and the old king will have to go."

There is a book by Morris West which is being read rather widely across the country entitled *The Shoes of the Fisherman.* One scene in the book vividly impressed me. An archbishop of the Catholic church was a political prisoner of the Russians. He was being held in a work camp located in the frozen wastelands of the far north. His release had been negotiated. Authorities relayed word of his freedom to him. He seemed reluctant to accept it. "Don't you want to be free?" he was asked. "I have been free a long, long time," he replied. He went on to explain that in the early years of his confinement he had brooded over his imprisonment; he was bitter and resentful. But gradually, he had discovered that a man can find opportunities for service wherever he is. He had ministered to other persons, offering love and concern for them in a place where there was no love. Little by little, he had found freedom even in his slavery.

I, for one, have not found this lesson to be easy, but I have found it to be true. The only antidote to the poisonous effects of fear and worry is the contentment of constructive effort. I am beginning

101

to learn that if each day is lived as it ought to be lived, then tomorrow will bring its proper harvest of serenity. Those who live this way seem to find peace no matter what happens. Those who do not, never find it. That appears to be the way it is.

# Friendship—The Way It Is

Matthew 7:1-5

Shortly after the riots on the Columbia University campus, a twenty-one-year-old man was arrested by police and charged with the willful destruction of university property. Questioned by a member of the New York City Crime Commission, the man admitted that only a few weeks before he had come to the campus from another troubled college on the West Coast. Commenting on his reasons for participating in the confusion, he revealed an interesting insight into the basic loneliness of his own life. "Man, we've had it," he said. "We're uptight about being nobodies, as if we came from nowhere, belong to nothing, and nobody caring where we go. We gotta belong, man, we gotta belong!"

103

Despite other faults the lad may have had, he cannot be blamed for his yearning to belong. Any description of the psychological structure of man lists the need for satisfying social relationships as a dominating personality drive. Years ago, John Donne, Dean of St. Paul's Cathedral in London, preached a famous sermon. You will remember that in that sermon Donne declared, "No man is an island entire of himself." All of us belong to the great *continent of humanity.* This appears to be an accurate statement of the way things are. Any attempt to cut ourselves off from the rest of our brothers is to work against the intended scheme of things.

This is the reason that men, across the ages, have been intent on finding ways and means of building bridges between human beings. The desire to be accepted by our brothers is one of our native impulses. This, of course, explains so much of our behavior. We will sacrifice anything, including life itself, to gain the approval of our brothers. There is nothing sinful about this pursuit. When you and I attempt to find a way to belong, we are only doing what we were intended to do.

Jesus was aware of this innate drive; consequently, when he addressed himself to the problems of our existence, it was only natural that he concerned himself with it. Perhaps it was in response to a question from some lonely listener, who asked, "Master, how can I find a friend, a sense of belonging in this fragmented, separated world?" that Jesus laid down the words of our text. "Judge not, that ye be not judged. For with what judgment you judge, you will be judged. Don't look for the defect in your brother's eye until you consider your own." These are strange words. What do you suppose Jesus meant?

I

The first thing that seems significant in this text is that Jesus instructs us to begin the search for acceptance by demanding something of ourselves.

Scholars have long since agreed that the Sermon on the Mount is not in the truest sense a sermon. That is to say, Jesus did not offer this discourse on a single occasion. There is good reason to believe that the scribes who recorded these passages gleaned them from throughout the ministry of Jesus and assembled them as a sort of summary of the total message of his lifetime. It is, therefore, reasonable to assume that each portion of this sermon resulted from a particular situation faced by his listeners.

What circumstance could have given rise to

these words? Perhaps Jesus saw within his people a basic loneliness. They were trying to get together and could not find a way. "Look," said Jesus, "you are going at this thing the wrong way. You are trying to win the acceptance of your brothers by forcing their respect. This will never work. You must win their approval. You must begin with yourselves." This took them by surprise! They had never dreamed that separation from their brothers was their own fault.

It takes us by surprise, too. A lot is being said these days about the generation gap. If we were able to look at it impartially, it would be difficult to fix the blame. We hear the older generation talking about the irresponsibility of youth, their ungratefulness for the sacrifices of those who have gone before, and their careless disregard for authority. On the other side, we hear the youth talking about the hypocrisy of their elders, the failure of parents to understand their children, and the determination of the establishment to hold the status quo. How often do we hear either side attempting an honest appraisal of itself? We keep on trying to close the gap by judging the sins of the other side.

What do you suppose would happen in this splintered, divided world if all of us sat down together somewhere and admitted our own mis-

takes? Suppose young people were to confess that
they have not properly appreciated the great heri-
tage of the past and the sacrifices of their parents,
and that often they have been irresponsible and
careless? Suppose we admitted to our children
that we are guilty of hypocrisy and that we are
nothing more than human beings, capable of being
wrong as often as we are right? What do you suppose would happen to the gereration gap, to fami-
lies estranged from one another, if we stopped
blaming one another and started looking at ourselves?

The church of today seems to have degenerated
into a Society for the Confession of One Another's
Sins. This, of course, is not the way it was intended. To some degree, however, this is the way
it has turned out to be. The pulpit surely holds
a charter membership in that society. Preachers are
notoriously guilty of confessing the sins of laymen; and laymen are equally adept at confessing
the sins of the clergy. As a consequence, there is an
ever-widening estrangement between the pulpit
and the pew. What do you suppose would happen if we could recover the concept of the early
church? The first Christians gathered to confide
in one another, unashamed to admit that they
were imperfect people. As a result, the early

107

church was a dynamic, united force that swept
across the world.

## II

Second, Jesus was stating a basic law of creation:
life earns its corresponding reaction. For a moment, look again at the proposition from which we
are attempting to study the Sermon on the Mount.
History has questioned a lot of things about Jesus,
but never for long has man debated the validity
of his ethical teachings. Whether we like what he
said or not, there is the solid conviction that he
was right. The reason for this is evident. This man
understood the scheme of life. He looked deeply
into the nature of things, and then he gathered the
people around him—in the marketplace, in the
fields, by the seashore, and on the Mount of Olives
—and said to them, "This is how it is." When
we talk about the revelation of Jesus, this is part
of what we mean. Jesus described for us the nature
of life—the way it works.

One of the things Jesus talked most about was
the reciprocating tendency of creation, or the trend
in nature to reproduce its kind. He talked about
it at every level. "One day," he said, "a farmer
sowed some wheat. But that night an enemy
slipped into the fields and planted tares, and tares

108

and wheat both came up together. The wheat seed produced wheat, and the tares came up tares." The people must have nodded their heads in agreement. They knew about the law of wheat and tares. "Now," said Jesus, "let's move up to a higher level. Judge not, that you be not judged. For the judgment you give will be the judgment you receive." It is the same principle working on different levels. What a man does with this life, life does back to him. We have never managed to escape that principle.

Albert Schweitzer, in his book *Peace or Atomic War,* made a strong statement when he raised his voice in protest against the madness of the nuclear arms race. "He who uses atomic weapons to defend freedom would become subject to a similar fate." Not even the military leaders of the world would deny this. We are fully convinced that any nation foolish enough to sow the seeds of nuclear disaster would reap a like harvest. Is it not true that the total experience of history stands squarely behind what Jesus said in the Sermon on the Mount? What you give out, you eventually get.

This is the reason why Jesus insisted that we begin with ourselves in seeking the acceptance of our brother. We cannot hope to have the respect of our neighbor unless we have earned it. We can never expect to have his friendship until we have

109

offered him ours. An old story tells of a man whose wife sent him next door to borrow a saucepan. He came home battered and bruised, complaining that his neighbor had beat him up. His wife asked for an explanation. He explained that on his way over he began to mull over the possible negative attitudes with which he might be met at the neighbor's door. "He'll probably be watching the football game on TV. The doorbell will annoy him. He doesn't know me, and very likely he won't want me for a friend. Stupid guy, he won't even give me a chance." So when the door opened, the man shouted, "You bum, I didn't want your doggone saucepan anway."

A foolish story. But is it not true that many of us believe we receive shabby treatment in life simply because there is something wrong with the other guy? Jesus set the whole matter in a different perspective. "Begin with yourself. It may be that what you are getting back is nothing more than you are giving."

## III

Finally, observe how this principle of self-improvement affects human relationships. The last verse in our lesson reads: "First, remove the plank from your own eye, and then you can see clearly

110

to remove the speck of dust from your brother's eye." Most commentaries suggest that Jesus intentionally used this exaggeration to focus clearly what he was saying. The largest barriers to satisfying personal relationships are within ourselves.

I saw a comment the other day that had not occurred to me before. "The world generally hates its reformers but it has always loved its saints. And the reason for this is that the reformer concentrates on the sins of others while the saint concentrates on his own." There is enough truth here to merit some consideration. The people who have made the greatest impact for good on the course of human affairs have always started with themselves. They have won the admiration of mankind not so much by what they said, but by what they were.

There is a lesson here for the church in our times. Sometimes I suspect that we are trying to change the world with men who have not been changed themselves. As a consequence, we have lost the admiration and respect of the people outside the church. Now I am not advocating that the church lessen its concern about the great evils that afflict modern man. I am suggesting that we heighten the demands that we make on ourselves. We would feel considerably closer to that young man in New York City if he matched his desire to belong with creative and responsible action, instead of engaging in premeditated vandalism.

In Birmingham, Alabama, a small statue stands amidst a busy city street. It is one of the few public monuments in this country erected to the memory of a minister. I read the biography of this man the other day.[1] He was known across the state of Alabama as Brother Bryan. Brother Bryan was the pastor of a little church in Birmingham, but he was minister to the entire city. The story of his life sparkles with the love and grace of a true servant of God. He loved people, regardless of who they were or where he found them. The most wretched man in the city was his friend. He was never harsh in his evaluation of people no matter how evil they were. Brother Bryan sweetened the atmosphere of the city not because he was a reformer, but because he was a saint. I have been thinking a lot about this recently. Perhaps the place to begin changing the world is in the church. And who makes up the church? Is it you—or I?

[1] Hunter B. Blakely, *Religion in Shoes* (Richmond, Va.: John Knox Press, 1934).

# Prayer—The Way It Is

*Matthew 7:7-11*

Very early in life I read two of the most widely known adventure stories for boys ever published in our country. Written by Mark Twain, *Tom Sawyer* and *The Adventures of Huckleberry Finn* made a deep impression on my life. In those early years, I saw these books as the author's attempt to entertain young readers. Later I came to recognize them as Twain's serious reflections on some of the religious and social attitudes of his day. There is one passage in *Huckleberry Finn* that I have remembered. Huck tells of an attempt on the part of Miss Watson to teach him to pray. She "took me into the closet and prayed," he said, "but nothing come of it. She told me to pray every day and whatever I asked for I would get it. But it warn't so. I tried it."

## THERE'S NO OTHER WAY

The thought reflected in this passage seems to describe much of the contemporary attitude on a practice that is as old as man himself. Where man first conceived the notion of prayer is lost in the dusty records of antiquity. The earliest recorded histories of civilization reveal ancient formulas designed to influence the gods on man's behalf. Through the centuries, the notion of prayer has persisted, universally, as a part of man's life. Perhaps in modern times as at no other period in history we have come to question the basic validity of the idea itself. The notion of an orderly world where events happen by natural law has shaken our faith in prayer and all but eliminated our sense of need for it.

It is this modern skepticism which has raised serious doubt about one passage in the Sermon on the Mount. For the most part, we read the Sermon and accept the truth of it even though we do not practice it. However, there is at least one portion of it that appears to be absolutely unreasonable. One day Jesus said: "Ask, and it will be given you; seek, and you will find; knock, and it will be opened to you. What man of you, if his son asks for bread, will give him a stone, or if he asks for a fish, will give him a serpent? If you, then, being evil, know how to give good gifts, how much more will your Heavenly Father give good

things to those who ask him?" No person steeped
in the scientific atmosphere of the twentieth century can read these words without raising a question. We are likely to conclude that either Jesus
was unenlightened about the way things are, or we
do not understand what he said. If he was suggesting that whatever we pray for we can have,
he was wrong. Many of us have tried it, and it just
is not so. What was Jesus saying?

**I**

When you analyze this passage, two or three
principles are apparent. For one thing, Jesus is
emphasizing the wisdom of God's giving and not
his indiscriminate willingness to give. Now I understand that this is inconsistent with the meaning so
often ascribed to this passage; but we must deal
honestly with this whole matter of prayer if we are
to find it a meaningful practice in our spiritual
lives. Probably the greatest barrier to intelligent
faith in our times is our chronic unwillingness to
think through an idea to its basic meanings in the
light of existing knowledge. No place is this more
evident than in our understanding of this passage
on prayer. Jesus said, "Ask, and you shall receive."
And most often we close the book on this, believing that it is the final word on prayer. We

bow our heads, place an order at the cosmic department store, and, when delivery isn't made on schedule, we are bewildered to the point of losing our faith.

But, you see, the passage does not end with this one phrase. Jesus goes on to use an interesting illustration which qualifies his initial promise. "Not even an earthly father," he said, "will respond unwisely to a child's request. How much more can we expect the Divine Mind to manage his affairs with perfect wisdom." This comment of Jesus has not been adequately considered in our concept of prayer. If there is anything to prayer at all, it must include not only man's asking, but a place for God's wisdom in responding to man's request.

Surely there is nothing unreasonable abut this. Think what a colossal mess this world would be if God ran his universe subject to the whim of imperfect man. One man prays for rain so that his garden will grow; another prays for sunshine so that he may work in his garden. They live on the same street and in the same block. Even I can understand that the Almighty would have a problem if he gave to each of us a blank check. Some things have to be handled in an orderly fashion— the prayers of men notwithstanding.

One of Mark Twain's most biting and incisive

116

essays was printed in a little book that he allowed
to be published only after his death. Its title is
*The War Prayer*.[1] The book is a mythical account
of a minister's congregational prayer during a time
of war. The prayer was shot through with selfish
superpatriotism. "God help our side and never
mind the rest." At the close of the minister's prayer
that Sunday morning, a stranger entered the
church, took the pulpit, and addressed the people, saying that two prayers had been prayed that
day, one spoken, one unsaid. He charged that their
prayer for unqualified victory in battle suggested
a disregard for the welfare of their foes and that
unwittingly they had asked God to bless them and
to curse their enemies. Twain was sometimes un-
justifiably cynical and harsh in his estimate of
man's religious attitudes, but his lesson is not
without its point. If God remains consistent with
his character, he can never answer my prayer if
it must be answered at your expense, nor could
he conform to my requests by ignoring the total
good of all men.

What do you suppose would happen to so
much of our praying if we fully considered this? It
would mean that a selfish prayer is impossible.
We have no right to ask it, nor does God have a
right to answer it.

[1] (New York: Harper & Row, 1923).

## II

For another thing, prayer involves more than asking. It involves cooperative living.

Jesus used three words to describe prayer. The first was *ask*. Doubtless he recognized that this would be misunderstood. Talk is cheap. If he left his followers with the impression that God was at the command of those who placed their orders and stood by for delivery, they would soon become disillusioned about the whole business of praying. So he used two other words, *seek* and *knock*. These two words are more intense in meaning. They involve struggle and effort.

The simplest and most elementary implication of these two words is that God stands ready to serve us when we cooperate with him. This is an obvious reality. There is a story about a man who took his son fishing. The man told his son to pray for their success. They set their hooks and after a while went back to check them. They were loaded with fish. This went on for several hours. But finally they pulled in their lines and found them empty. "Did you pray?" asked the father. "No, I didn't," said the boy. "And why not?" insisted the man. "I remembered that we forgot to bait the hooks." That, it seems to me, is a fair description of the way prayer works.

118

I suspect that the most serious distortion that we have imposed on the concept of prayer is limiting it to words. Prayer must also involve the seeking out of God's laws, being obedient to them, and then waiting for the certain and trustworthy processes of the universe to answer back, supplying our needs and providing for our necessities. Edward West wrote, "I confess to having spent half my life being outraged and concerned over human difficulties and wishing that something could be done about them, only to discover that the somebody called to do something about them was the tired, outraged, concerned man doing the praying—myself." [2] I wonder if we are not praying when we allow our lives, wherever we work and live, to reflect the spirit of Christ? Is it not prayer when we lift a fallen man, assist a helpless child, offer encouragement to the hopeless, and minister to the needs of suffering humanity?

If we are accused of robbing prayer of some of its mystery, then we must plead guilty. As long as we confine prayer to the recitation of requests in Old English, we can expect to be, like Huckleberry Finn, compeletely disillusioned with its meaning. God has his own way of doing things. We have fallen into a curious kind of reasoning

[2] Edward N. West, *God's Image in Us* (Cleveland and New York: World Publishing Co., 1960), p. 132.

when we imagine that God's response to prayer must always be associated with the supernatural. It seems to me that I am praying when I visit my doctor and take the medicine he prescribes for my illness. It isn't the doctor or the drug that makes me well. It is God working through them. Prayer, in its widest meaning, is a way of living. It is seeking, knocking, persistently attempting to find the will of God, and responding cooperatively to it. And this principle prevails with regard not only to my physical health, but to my mental, spiritual, and emotional well-being.

## III

Finally, prayer is a means by which God is able to do for us what he could not do otherwise. Jesus ended his comment on the nature of prayer with these words: "Your Heavenly Father will give you good things if you ask him." I suspect that Jesus, the day he stood talking to his disciples about this matter of praying, underscored the word *if*. For without that word, the inherent freedom of man would be denied. Our reception of God's gifts is ultimately dependent upon our willingness to receive them. Man is potentially capable of hiding from every blessing of God, including life itself. Conversely, we are also capable of being the recipients of his unlimited gifts. The conditional factor is the degree of our willingness to receive.

Let me use a homely illustration: One cold February day, I was standing at my study window mulling over the meaning of this scripture lesson. I saw a mother and her child emerge from their car and turn down the street. The child was without a coat. Even from my vantage point I could see the little fellow shiver and clap his hands to keep warm. The mother held in her hands a warm, woolen jacket. She called to the little boy to come get his coat. But his attention was focused down the street. The boy moved so rapidly that his mother could not catch him. She stood there with the coat, willing to put it on him, but the stubborn little boy was unwilling to receive it. It seemed to me that here was a clue to the meaning of this text. God's goodness is limited only by our unwillingness to receive. Prayer is the opening of ourselves to God.

This makes the potential power of prayer unlimited, does it not? I heard someone say the other day, "I had a talk with God this morning." Our first reaction to this is to mark this person down as a religious nut. But I wonder. Perhaps this person has simply gone beyond the place where most of us are and become so sensitive to the spirit of God that two-way conversation is possible. H. G. Wells once said, "At times, in the silence of the night, and in rare lonely moments, I experience a sort of communion of myself with Something Great that is not myself."

Approach it this way. During my freshman year in college, I stumbled inadvertently into a class on calculus. I thought I was in the right place so I found a chair and began to listen. It took me only a few seconds to realize that this was far beyond me. I managed to slip out quietly and go down the hall to the place where the common people met—a class in freshman math. I felt more at home there, so I stayed. I report with some pride that I finally managed to make it to that class on calculus. By the time I had worked my way up through the ranks, I was tuned in on their wavelength and could understand at least part of what was being said.

Who knows what the capacities of man really are? Someday we may be able to bridge the gap of space and time in unbelievable ways, far beyond our present mechanical devices. We may discover that the problem of disease is not physical, but emotional or psychological, and healing may become a way of thinking. Someday we may become so attuned to the world of the spirit that we can converse with God in his own tongue. Some people seem to have touched this unseen world, only lightly and momentarily, perhaps, but enough to know that it is real. Without exception, these are people who have understood that prayer is not just asking, but seeking, probing, and persistent knocking. These people are unanimous in their testimony. If you ask, God will answer—in his own way, but he will answer.

# Religion—The Way It Is

*Matthew 7:17-23*

In Arlington, Virginia, a large church recently sent a questionnaire to its members, asking them to evaluate the effectiveness of its work. An unusually large number of people responded to the request, giving the church some rather interesting insights into the attitudes of its congregation. One section of the questionnaire was set aside for an evaluation of the meaning of the church in the people's lives. On the whole, the response was encouraging. There were, however, a number of members who marked these blanks, "Dull, boring, and irrelevant."

This experience could probably be duplicated in almost any church. There are many people, both in and out of the church, who feel that it is drab, dull, and lifeless. A little boy asked his minister about a plaque with a list of names that was on the wall of the church. "Those are the members of the church," said the minister, "who died in service." "Which service," asked the tired little fellow, "the eight forty-five, or the eleven o'clock?" I think I know what he meant. The church is often dull, unexciting, and dreary, and I have done more than my share in making it that way.

However, while the church is often lifeless and dehydrated, the Christian faith ought not to be. There is a marked difference among people bearing the Christian label. There are some who are alive, excited, and radiant, drawing on their faith like deep wells of water. There are others who are glum, despondent, and depressed, dragging their religion along like so much excess baggage. What makes the difference? It seems to me that at least part of the answer can be found in this passage from the Great Sermon.

Jesus said, "Not everyone who says to me, 'Lord, Lord,' shall enter the kingdom of heaven, but he who does the will of my Father." For many years I saw this passage as an attempt on the part of Jesus to scold his followers for their infidelity. More recently, I have come to see it as a statement of one of life's basic principles. Let us think about it for a moment.

# I

Let us begin by making two preliminary observations: The first concerns the expression "the kingdom of heaven." This phrase appears often in the Bible, and, for the most part, we attach the "other world" meaning to it. I am not altogether sure this is valid. While it cannot be disassociated completely from the afterlife, we do not have to wait for death to open for us the gates to abundant life. To believe that his world is a prison, and that man is condemned to a miserable existence as long as he is a part of it, is both unreasonable and unchristian. Jesus often talked about the immediacy of the kingdom of heaven. "The kingdom of God is within you," he said on one occasion. On another, he declared, "Whosoever believeth hath eternal life." The verb is in the present tense, not the future. This leads us to conclude that heaven can be both a present and future reality. Life can be exciting, meaningful, and radiant not only later, but here and now.

The other thing that concerns us about the traditional interpretation of this passage is that we have taken it to be a threat. It is clear why this has happened. Certain lines in this passage contain some hard words. Jesus appears to be saying that God will ultimately even the score with those of us who talk a good game and never play it. This, I submit, is inconsistent with the rest of the Gospel. Imagine a father who sits off observing the infidelity of his children, and, finally, in a spirit of angry revenge, pounces upon them and settles the account. This is not the image of God that Jesus presents in the New Testament, and to picture him thus does violence to the Christian concept of the Father.

I think what Jesus is saying here is not a threat, but rather a statement of the way life is. Man is prohibited from entering the kingdom of heaven, not because God seeks revenge upon us for our disobedience, but rather because we cut ourselves out. Harry Emerson Fosdick preached a sermon once on the theme "Catching the Right Bus." He told of a man who wanted to go to Detroit but caught the bus to Kansas City. The inevitable consequence was that the man arrived in Kansas City. There is nothing unusual about this. We generally reach the destination to which the chosen road leads. It isn't God who keeps us from getting the right destination when we have chosen the wrong road. It is the way life works—the way it is.

A long time ago, Jesus recognized this. People were crowding eagerly around him demanding entrance to the kingdom of heaven. Their lives were miserable, full of despair and conflict. They wanted life to be different. They were tired of living on the edge of desperation, worried, anxious, and afraid. "Let us in," they demanded, "and we will call you 'Lord.'" But Jesus could not do it. "No," he said, "you cannot call me 'Lord, Lord' and enter the kingdom of heaven. You have to do the will of the Father." And from what we know about life and the way it works, we are compelled to agree that Jesus was telling it like it is! This is true for two reasons.

## II

The first is this: The mere profession of faith constitutes a drag on life. In our study of the Sermon on the Mount, we have agreed that it is not a sermon in the usually accepted sense. These sayings were gleaned from the total ministry of Jesus and assembled into one discourse by the New Testament writers. This explains the lack of unity in the sermon. I suspect this passage comes from near the end of his ministry. Jesus observed that so many of his followers had found no meaning in their profession of discipleship. They stood in the streets and cheered him as he passed, as they had done on his last entrance into Jerusalem that first Palm Sunday; but their lives were empty and their religion was dull, drab, and irrelevant. Perhaps it was against this background that Jesus stopped and said to them in deep compassion, "I want you to have the kind of life that you long to have, but you will never have it as long as you limit your allegiance to the mere confession of my name."

Surely our experience stands squarely behind this fact. Observing the mechanics of religion without practicing its teachings constitutes a serious and tiresome burden. Several years ago, an enterprising reporter looking for a story wandered through the streets of an eastern city watching the faces of the people on their way to church. "I was struck," he said, "by the expressions of misery on so many faces. I got the idea that they were being driven to the church by a sense of duty, that they were constantly tormented by the feeling that they were missing something they had rather be doing." Perhaps this reporter was overly imaginative, but it is true that a faith confined to the church is a bothersome thing. If we have not attempted to live out our faith on the street, then the formal exercises of the faith will be largely meaningless. Someone has rightly said, "*Church* religion is just enough to make us miserable."

I once read a story about a plow that was sent to Africa some years ago. It fell into the hands of a primitive tribe in the interior of the continent. The people had never seen such an instrument before. Not knowing what to do with it, they set it up in their fields and worshiped it. Each day they would interrupt their work for prayers. The plow, of course, was designed to cultivate the soil and provide food. However, instead of its being used as a means of deliverance for the people, it became an added burden in their lives.

This kind of thing has happened often in other ways. I do not completely discount the value of practicing the mechanics of religion. There is some virtue, I suppose, in simply going through the exercise of prayer, the study of the Bible, and the repeating of creeds. But if we are determined not to apply the lessons of faith in the places where we work and play, then the exercises of faith will always be a chore. This is what Jesus is saying here. You are going to miss the kingdom of heaven not only in the hereafter, but also in the here and now, if you only *call* me Lord and do not the things I command you to do. Failure to allow a tree to produce its fruit is to render the tree useless. Religion limited to the surface is dull, boring, and burdensome. We have to take it out of the church if it is to have any meaning.

## III

The second reason for Jesus' statement is this: It is the practice of our faith that gives it meaning.

One of the oldest preacher stories in the world is about two ministers who were being considered by a congregation to serve as their pastor. The congregation decided to ask each of them to read the twenty-third Psalm and then to make their decision. One of the men was a polished speaker, capable in every detail of proper diction and emphasis, but a man without convictions and compassion. The other was an average speaker, but a man sincerely dedicated and deeply committed. They read the words, "The Lord is my shepherd, . . ." The congregation turned in its verdict and called the latter. "The first man," they said, "knew the psalm. The second knew the shepherd."

It makes a difference when you know the shepherd. There is a decided contrast in the way people worship, even in the way they sing the hymns of the church. In every congregation there are people who cannot sing, who are able to cover an entire hymn without even approximating the tune. Yet they participate with an enthusiasm that comes from their hearts. I have had the privilege of knowing some of these people personally, and, in every case, they sing because the words have great meaning for them. They have been out there in the middle of things where the going is rough. They have attempted to live out their faith, test it in every situation, and apply it to every circumstance.

131

To them, the hymns are no longer just poetry set to music, but a factual testimony of the way they have found their faith to work. This leads us to believe that the relevance of worship is dependent not only upon what is done in the church, but also upon what we bring to it.

We can illustrate this in so many ways. The words of worship come alive only as we experience them. A friend, who is a minister, was returning home one night from a meeting. The rain was falling in torrents. The car skidded on a curve and smashed down a steep embankment. The minister's wife was killed. He was hospitalized for days, but on the first Sunday back in his pulpit he said to his congregation, "Many times I have exhorted you to cast your burdens on the Lord, promising you that he would sustain you. I believed it then but never as I do now."

Here is one of life's most valuable insights. Nowadays so many people are demanding meaning in religion. Could it be that the problem is not so much what goes on in church, but what we do with it afterward? The power of love, for instance, is never evident in our world simply because we talk about it in church. Its meaning only becomes evident as we apply it on the street. We will never know much about the love of God simply by referring to it in our creeds. Somewhere along the

132

way we have to surrender to God—lean on the everlasting arms—before it ever becomes real.

On a bright morning long ago, Jesus came back to Jerusalem for the final time. The people met him in the streets, proclaiming him to be their Lord. "Give us the kingdom of heaven now," they cried, "and we will make you king." But Jesus could not give it to them. He could only tell them how to find it. "It is not the man who calls me 'Lord' who finds the kingdom of heaven. It is the man who does my Father's will." From what we know about life, this appears to be the way it is. Today would be a good day to take Jesus seriously!

# Life—The Way It Is

*Matthew 5:48*

Some time ago there was a story in *Newsweek* about a man in California who has founded a new religious movement known as the Universal Life Church, Inc. The founder is a fifty-seven-year-old former North Carolinian described by the magazine as highly illiterate. The movement he has established is unique, to say the least. "Our church don't have no doctrine," he is quoted as saying. "That's what people all over the world like about it. The thing that's putting America in the graveyard is a little black book called the Holy Bible." The story reports that the West Coast hippies find the new movement attractive. The founder stands for free love and the use of psychedelic drugs, and assumes a solid antiestablishment pose. The headquarters for his church is now being housed in his garage, where a ten-man force is required to handle his mail.

At first glance, most of us are rather shocked that a movement such as this could gain any support among the thoughtful people in our times. Yet when we think about it carefully, we can half understand why this sort of thing would attract attention. One of the problems of the Christian faith is that it proclaims a system of ethics that appears to be unrealistic for human achievement. Throughout the ages, the critics of our faith have insisted that Jesus demands too much of his followers. Anyone who takes him seriously is likely to find the strain of reaching the perfection he demanded too much for human abilities. To a degree, this criticism is understandable. Someone has described the Sermon on the Mount as the Mount Everest of ethics. In this three-chapter treatise in Matthew's Gospel, Jesus suggests principles for living which are so radically different from natural human impulses that they appear impossible. As a consequence, there is a wide disenchantment with the Christian ethic. We are prone to accept another system more consistent with our abilities.

It is not at all uncommon these days to hear someone say that the demands Jesus makes of us cannot be achieved in our kind of world. A businessman wonders if he can meet competition and observe the Golden Rule. A college student admitted to her counselor that, while a committed Christian in her ideals, she found it necessary to keep her allegiance a secret. "No one believes," she said, "that you can be Christian and be realistic on today's college campus." All of us, to some degree, share her concern. Jesus demanded perfection in our lives, and we wonder if, where we live and work, this is possible.

The following question has been chosen as the theme for our final study in the Sermon on the Mount. Stated precisely, the question is: "Why should we cling to the visionary ideals of that long-ago dreamer?" Clearly we are unable to achieve what he asked of us. If we cannot reach it, then why not forget it?

# I

We can begin by remembering that a high goal is necessary for growth in life. You remember, perhaps, the story about a mountaineer who achieved a wide reputation as a marksman with a rifle. The forests around his home were filled with trees covered with circles drawn in chalk. In the exact center of every circle there was a bullet hole. The entire community was impressed with his ability. What they did not know was that the man shot first and then drew a circle around the bullet hole. This, of course, is one way to establish a reputation for marksmanship. But it hardly increases the skill of the marksman.

One approach to this whole matter of ethics gives us concern. James Armstrong in *The Journey That Men Make* refers to a college textbook which defines morality as "the quality of behaving in a way society approves." This means, I suppose, that what we ought to do is equivalent to what we are doing. This idea carried to its ultimate extreme, as Armstrong so aptly points out, means that cannibalism is moral for cannibals and the slaughter of the Jews was moral in the Third Reich.

One of the problems in establishing ideals as identical with custom is that it provides no incentive for improving life. Consider how impoverished our world would be if man had been content to move on this level. Certainly there would have been no achievement in the field of science. How can we explain the development of the wheel, the invention of writing, and the discovery of medicine except that long ago someone believed that there was a difference between what life was and what it could be? The great social revolutions, such as those that liberated women from a place of

137

menial servitude, took children out of the coal
mines of Europe, and released slaves from their
bondage, have resulted from the dreams of ideal-
ists, who had a vision beyond that which they
had attained, and who refused to accept custom
as the final standard of behavior. The progress of
man has always been in direct proportion to the
dreams he has had beyond his reach, and the
discontent in his heart, which, has lifted him from
what he *is* to what he knows he *ought* to be.

John Baillie refers in his book *To Whom Shall
We Go?* to a sentence written by the great Swedish
explorer, Nansen. "What would life be without its
dreams?" In early life Nansen had dreamed of
opening the unknown areas of the world by ex-
ploration and, in later life, he actually charted the
vast regions of the North Pole. Still later, at the
close of the First World War, his dreams took
him into the service of the refugees of Europe.

It seems to me that we should consider such
outgrowths of idealism before we mark off the
demands of Jesus as unrealistic. Jesus could, of
course, have simply lowered his sights and laid
down ideals which were within the grasp of his
immediate disciples. But he chose to speak to
the ages and to set before us the ideals established
by the Councils of Eternity. Perhaps they lie beyond our immediate grasp. Perhaps we can never

love as we ought to love; perhaps we can never fully forgive those who spitefully use us, or perhaps we can never honestly pray the Lord's Prayer; but, unless we have a dream that exceeds our grasp, what motivation do we have for growth? The most deadly predicament for any person is to reach the point when his dreams meet his achievements and he no longer struggles.

## II

While the ethics of the Sermon on the Mount may lie beyond our immediate grasp, the struggle to achieve them gives direction to our lives. In the early years of my life, a quotation from Emerson was popular: "Hitch your wagon to a star." In more recent years, we have become disillusioned with this idea. Psychologists suggest that when there is too great a difference between what we are and what we aspire to become, emotional and mental breakdown can result. This may be true, but I noted a comment the other day which could merit some thought, at least. "Hitching your wagon to a star may be too high a goal, but at least it will keep you out of the ditch."

It seems to me that it is always better to aim too high than too low. One of the things I have tried to underline in our study of the Sermon on the

Mount is that if life is to become what it was intended to be, then it must conform to the principles suggested here. And to the degree that we fail to make application of these principles, our lives will be frustrated, empty, and incomplete. It would appear, therefore, that the person who struggles to attain high ideals will find a more meaningful and abundant life than the person who simply makes no effort at all.

The apostle Paul was one of those rare souls in history who had one consuming ideal. "For me to live is Christ," he said. He was fully aware that the pattern was too big for him. He admitted this. "I count not myself to have arrived," he declared in one of his letters, "but this one thing I do, I press on." He never managed achievements to equal his dreams, but those dreams gave a direction to his life that has enabled him to dominate much of the religious thinking of the past two thousand years.

One of the things that trouble me most about our day is that the difficulty we have in maintaining a Christian commitment has dissuaded us from making any commitment at all. I recognize the problem in approximating the ideals of the Sermon on the Mount. I have a deep sympathy for the businessman who lives in eternal tension between the necessity for profit at any price and the determination not to sell his soul. I sense the predicament of the present-day youth who still believes in purity of character and the integrity of conscience. That youngster has no place to hide and must live every day of his life on the front lines. Even the minister spends his life in conflict between what he believes he must do to survive popular opinion and what he has to do to fulfill the obligations of his calling. I do not know anyone who is having an easy time battling the tide in this runaway, crazy world. But to abandon an ideal simply because it is a difficult goal seems to be an invitation to disaster. Life has a greater meaning for those who try and fail than it does for those who never try at all.

Consider the dreams of those who have made great contributions to life. Michael Faraday is an outstanding example. His notebook was filled with hundreds of notations about the failures in his experiments. Undoubtedly, he dreamed of a world which would one day move on the power of electromagnetic energy. Faraday died before the days of computers, guided missiles, air-conditioning, and television, but his dreams enabled him to do something. One day in 1831, this blacksmith's son—a onetime newsboy—while working in his laboratory, stumbled across a precious secret. He had succeeded at last in converting magnetic force

141

into usable electric energy. This discovery is a landmark event in human history. It illustrates that a person who reaches for the stars will usually accomplish something worthwhile. He will rise higher than those who never reach for anything.

## III

Finally, while a high ideal may be beyond our grasp, the pursuit of it does unify life. There is a need these days for a lot of preaching on the necessity of decision in the achieving of a meaningful life. It seems to me that one of the things creating so much turmoil, tension, and turbulence in our lives is that we are trying to walk down too many roads at the same time. Not long ago, a lady was trying to buy a hat in a department store. She had about the most pained expression that I have ever seen. Hats were scattered everywhere, and she was asking for more. My wife explained her predicament. She wanted a single hat that would make her look slimmer but not taller, dressy but not formal, inexpensive but not cheap, that would be appropriate for both funerals and weddings, and that would match anything. No wonder she was in a quandary! You always are when your dreams are in conflict with each other and your ideals are contradictory. Jesus under-

142

stood this. Consequently, he set before the ages a single standard of life. "Your only hope of finding peace," he said in effect, "is to take your stand under a single flag and surrender to a principle great enough to command your highest allegiance."

This is why the California minister's Universal Life Church will probably never catch the permanent attention of man. A church without a doctrine sounds exciting enough. But if a man does not believe anything, then he has nothing by which to chart direction. As a result, he drives himself to distraction, wandering around on the misty flats of indecision.

Several years ago *Redbook* magazine published a novel about a young minister who had been assigned to his first parish. Shortly after his arrival, a crisis arose, forcing him to take a stand. The voices tugging at him were many. There was, of course, the position of the majority of his parishioners, daring him to stand in defiance. There was the welfare of his family, who stood to suffer greatly if his position proved unpopular. His own professional pride demanded a decision that he could successfully defend. Finally, there was the clear voice of conscience burning deep within his soul. All of these voices were in conflict, and between them he had to choose.

## THERE'S NO OTHER WAY

All of us live on such a battlefield, and there comes a time when a decision has to be made. The problem of life is to choose an ideal that will not fail. Two thousand years ago, the Supreme Teacher of the ages stood on a faraway hilltop and laid down a carefully conceived plan of life. Since that long-ago day, his words have been tested in all the fires of human experience. The common witness of history has judged his proposal for life to be consistent with God's intended plan. No man since that day has managed to match his life completely with that proposal. But those who have turned their faces in that direction and struggled to attain the heights whisper back to the rest of us, "This is the life that God intended all men to have."